Demystifying the First Year of Law School

ASPEN PUBLISHERS

Demystifying
the First Year of Law School: A Guide to the 1L Experience

ALBERT J. MOORE

Professor of Law, University of California, Los Angeles

and

DAVID A. BINDER

Professor of Law, University of California, Los Angeles

Wolters Kluwer

Law & Business

AUSTIN   BOSTON   CHICAGO   NEW YORK   THE NETHERLANDS

Aspen Publishers
Attn: Permissions Department
76 Ninth Avenue, 7th Floor
New York, NY 10011-5201

To contact Customer Care, e-mail customer.care@aspenpublishers.com,
call 1-800-234-1660, fax 1-800-901-9075, or mail correspondence to:

Aspen Publishers
Attn: Order Department
PO Box 990
Frederick, MD 21705

Printed in the United States of America.

1 2 3 4 5 6 7 8 9 0

ISBN 978-0-7355-8449-5

Library of Congress Cataloging-in-Publication Data

Moore, Albert J.
  Demystifying the first year of law school : a guide to the 1L experience /
Albert J. Moore and David A. Binder.
    p. cm.
  Includes index.
  ISBN 978-0-7355-8449-5
1. Law schools—United States. 2. Law students—United States. 3. Law—
Vocational guidance—United States. 4. Practice of law—United States. I.
Binder, David A. II. Title.

  KF283.M66 2009
  340.071'173—dc22

2009028666

About Wolters Kluwer Law & Business

Wolters Kluwer Law & Business is a leading provider of research information and workflow solutions in key specialty areas. The strengths of the individual brands of Aspen Publishers, CCH, Kluwer Law International and Loislaw are aligned within Wolters Kluwer Law & Business to provide comprehensive, in-depth solutions and expert-authored content for the legal, professional and education markets.

CCH was founded in 1913 and has served more than four generations of business professionals and their clients. The CCH products in the Wolters Kluwer Law & Business group are highly regarded electronic and print resources for legal, securities, antitrust and trade regulation, government contracting, banking, pension, payroll, employment and labor, and healthcare reimbursement and compliance professionals.

Aspen Publishers is a leading information provider for attorneys, business professionals and law students. Written by preeminent authorities, Aspen products offer analytical and practical information in a range of specialty practice areas from securities law and intellectual property to mergers and acquisitions and pension/benefits. Aspen's trusted legal education resources provide professors and students with high-quality, up-to-date and effective resources for successful instruction and study in all areas of the law.

Kluwer Law International supplies the global business community with comprehensive English-language international legal information. Legal practitioners, corporate counsel and business executives around the world rely on the Kluwer Law International journals, loose-leafs, books and electronic products for authoritative information in many areas of international legal practice.

Loislaw is a premier provider of digitized legal content to small law firm practitioners of various specializations. Loislaw provides attorneys with the ability to quickly and efficiently find the necessary legal information they need, when and where they need it, by facilitating access to primary law as well as state-specific law, records, forms and treatises.

Wolters Kluwer Law & Business, a unit of Wolters Kluwer, is headquartered in New York and Riverwoods, Illinois. Wolters Kluwer is a leading multinational publisher and information services company.

To Ethel Moore
  Still a constant source of love and inspiration.
    Albert

To Michael, Charles, and Jeffrey
  For greatly enriching my life.
    Uncle D

Summary of Contents

Contents

chapter 4

Six Types of Legal Arguments Commonly Used in Rule Application Cases

chapter 5

Reading Rule Application Opinions in Preparation for Class — Preparing a Case "Brief"

Acknowledgments

Many thanks to our research assistants Michael Chow, Katy Klinedinst, Whitney MacDonald, Kelly Perigoe, Damion Robinson, and Khaldoun Shobaki for all their hard work, helpful suggestions, and patience.

We shared a number of our ideas for this work with participants in the Clinical Theory Workshop, led by Stephen Ellmann of New York Law School. Debbie Maranville graciously hosted us at a faculty presentation at the University of Washington Law School. We thank the participants in both groups for their comments and feedback on earlier drafts of this book.

Our thanks to Frederic Bloom, Tamie Bryant, Jerry Kang, Jason Light, Eugene Volokh, and Pavel Wonsowicz, and to the many other members of the UCLA Law School for their feedback on earlier drafts of this book.

Special thanks to Jerry Lopez for the extensive feedback, insights, and static he gave us in the early stages of this project. You made us rethink the project from the ground up.

We would also like to thank the UCLA Academic Senate and Deans Michael Schill and Jonathan Varat for their encouragement and generous financial support.

Finally, to our long-suffering spouses, without your love, patience, and support this project would never have been completed.

Albert J. Moore
David A. Binder

Los Angeles, California
2009

Demystifying the First Year of Law School

chapter 1

Introduction

I. WHY READ THIS BOOK

In your first year of law school, you will probably take courses in contract law, tort law, property law, civil procedure, criminal law, and constitutional law. In each of these subjects, your classes will mainly focus on reading, discussing, and analyzing court opinions. You can observe this reality by glancing at your first-year textbooks. As you will see, these texts contain primarily, though not exclusively, court opinions.

To prepare for each of your classes, you will routinely be asked to read one or more court opinions. You will then go to class and discuss these opinions. From the class discussions of court opinions you should learn at least three centrally important matters.

First, you should learn to identify the "issue" or "issues" in an opinion. Second, an opinion usually provides a rationale for resolving an "issue"; you should learn how to analyze and critique this rationale. Finally, you should also learn many of the legal rules that govern the area of law on which your class is focused. For instance, in your contracts course, you should learn many of the legal rules that comprise the law of contracts.

The process through which you learn to identify "issues," analyze and critique the reasoning in an opinion, and learn the legal rules in an opinion is likely to be very different from the learning process in many of your undergraduate courses. In law school, professors are unlikely to explicitly tell you what you need to learn. Thus, a professor may not identify for you the "issue" in an opinion, the strengths and weaknesses in the court's rationale for resolving an "issue," or the legal rules you should learn from reading an opinion. Instead, your professors will routinely ask you or your classmates questions such as the following:

What is the issue faced by the court?

Why did the court resolve the issue as it did?

What legal rule is the court applying in this case?

Do you think the court reached the correct result?

What rationale might support a different result than that reached by the court?

Could the court have reached a different result? Would a different result have been preferable?

Although professors routinely pose these questions, they will frequently decline to answer them. You (and many of your fellow law students) may find that no clear answer to these questions emerges from either the opinion itself or the class dialogues and discussions about the opinion. As a result, you may find yourself mystified, frustrated, and asking yourself questions like the following:

Why does the professor primarily ask questions and often not answer questions? Why doesn't the professor tell me what I need to learn from the court's opinion? Why is the professor asking me and my friend Sally if the court reached the right result? Sally and I have been in law school for only a few weeks, how are we supposed to know if the court got it right? Why am I being asked to critique an opinion written by a judge who presumably knows the law? And when Harry in the front row answers a question from the professor, what am I supposed to do with his answer? (I've talked to Harry and he is more confused than I am.) Why is it that when class discussion does seem to settle on a correct answer to a question, the professor then immediately seeks a contrary view and makes that contrary view seem reasonable? If the professor knows what the issue is and whether the court resolved it correctly, why doesn't the professor just tell me the court was right or explain why the court was wrong? Why the runaround? What should I have learned from reading the opinion and discussing it in class?

This book is intended to help you answer these questions. The book explains how to read and analyze court opinions in preparation for class. It also sets out and analyzes concrete examples of classroom question-and-answer exchanges between professors and students. These sample dialogues, and the explanations that follow them, illustrate and explain what you should learn from listening to and participating in class discussions. The book also explains why professors frequently ask questions in class rather than simply telling you what you need to know. Finally, the book provides concrete examples and illustrations of how what you should learn from reading court opinions and discussing them in class will help you on law school exams and later in law practice.

II. THE ORGANIZATION OF THIS BOOK

Court opinions in every area of law (contracts, property, criminal law, etc.) typically resolve the following two types of legal issues:

Some court opinions resolve issues of **legal rule application**, i.e., the issue is whether the facts of a case satisfy or fail to satisfy the requirements of one or more legal rules.

Other court opinions resolve issues of **legal rule creation**, i.e., the issue is whether a court should create or adopt a new, broadly applicable legal rule, and, if so, what the new rule should be.

In some instances, a single court opinion will involve both issues of legal rule application and legal rule creation.

Part One of the book (Chapters 2–10) focuses on **legal rule application**. Part Two of the book (Chapters 11–13) focuses on **legal rule creation**. This part concludes with an analysis of an opinion that involves both legal rule **application** and legal rule **creation**.

Part Three of the book (Chapters 14–16) elaborates on some important concepts introduced in Part One and Part Two, explores the inherently subjective nature of judicial decision making and illustrates how the skills you learn in your first year will help you counsel clients in law practice.

part 1

Legal Rule Application

Chapter 2 provides an explanation of how to identify or "spot" issues when applying a legal rule to a set of facts. This chapter also explains that lawyers make arguments to try to persuade courts to resolve issues in their client's favor.

Chapter 3 provides you with an opportunity to practice your issue-spotting skills.

Chapter 4 provides illustrative examples of some of the arguments that are commonly made by lawyers, and used by courts, to resolve issues.

Chapter 5 explains how you should analyze rule application opinions in preparation for class.

Chapters 6–9 provide you with sample classroom question-and-answer dialogues. These chapters illustrate what you might learn from listening to and participating in classroom question-and-answer dialogues and discussions of rule application opinions. They also explain why professors routinely ask questions in class and frequently fail to provide definitive answers to questions.

chapter 2

Legal Rules, Legal Categories, and Issue Spotting

". . . [A]ny time we either produce or understand any utterances of any reasonable length, we are employing dozens if not hundreds of categories: categories of speech sounds, of words, of phrases and clauses, as well as conceptual categories. Without the ability to categorize, we could not function at all, either in the physical world or in our social and intellectual lives. An understanding of how we categorize is central to any understanding of how we think and how we function, and therefore central to an understanding of what makes us human."[1]

I. LEGAL RULES AND LEGAL CATEGORIES

One of the most basic skills you will learn in your first year of law school is how to apply one or more legal rules to a set of facts. The facts will typically come either from a court opinion or a hypothetical case provided by your professor. To acquire this skill, you first need to be able to break down legal rules into their component parts.

Your professors may use several different terms to refer to the component parts of legal rules. The component parts are sometimes called "elements," "requirements," "sub-elements," "factors," or "categories." Throughout this book, we will refer to the component parts of legal rules[2] as "categories."

---

1. George Lakoff, *Women, Fire, and Dangerous Things, What Categories Reveal about the Mind* 6 (U. of Chicago Press 1987).

2. As you are probably aware, legal rules come from a variety of sources. These sources include federal and state court opinions, state legislatures, Congress, and governmental agencies such as the Environmental Protection Agency. But all legal rules, regardless of their source, contain legal categories.

The following examples illustrate how legal rules might[3] be broken down into legal categories.

Legal Rule #1: A product is considered unsafe if it is defective in its design or manufacture and the defect renders it potentially harmful to those using the product in a reasonably foreseeable manner.

Legal Categories in the Rule: A product (Category 1) is considered unsafe if it is defective (Category 2) in its design (Category 3) or manufacture (Category 4) and the defect renders it potentially harmful (Category 5) to those using the product (Category 6) in a reasonably foreseeable manner (Category 7).

Legal Rule #2: Burglary is the breaking and entering into the dwelling of another person in the nighttime with the intent to commit a felony therein.

Legal Categories in the Rule: Burglary is the breaking (Category 1) and entering into (Category 2) the dwelling (Category 3) of another person (Category 4) in the nighttime (Category 5) with the intent to commit a felony (Category 6) therein (Category 7).

Identifying legal categories is important because **the application of legal rules proceeds category by category**. That is, when applying a legal rule to a set of facts, you (or a court) will routinely need to consider if the facts satisfy each category in the rule. Thus, for example, to determine if a person is guilty of burglary under the above rule, you (or a court) would consider whether the facts of a case fit within <u>each</u> of the categories in the rule.

To illustrate this category-by-category application of a legal rule, assume the following facts are true beyond a reasonable doubt: at 8:00 P.M. the defendant entered another person's house with the intent to assault an occupant of the house with a deadly weapon (assault with a deadly weapon is a felony) and the assault was to take place inside the house. These facts alone would <u>not</u> establish the crime of burglary under the above rule. Although these facts would satisfy Categories 2–7 in the rule, the facts do not establish that the defendant "broke into" the house. If there was no breaking into the house, Category 1 in the rule has not been satisfied and the defendant is not guilty of a burglary (although the defendant might be guilty of another crime).

---

3. We say "might" because reasonable judges, lawyers, and law professors can often disagree about exactly how to break down a legal rule into legal categories. You will develop techniques and strategies for breaking legal rules into categories as you progress through the first year of law school.

II. LEGAL CATEGORIES AND LEGAL ISSUES

As you proceed category by category when applying a legal rule, you will find that it is sometimes obvious that the facts of a case or a hypothetical clearly satisfy or fail to satisfy a particular legal category. For example, if a defendant breaks down a locked door to a house with a sledgehammer to gain entrance, those facts would clearly satisfy the legal category of "breaking in" in the burglary rule above. On the other hand, if a defendant is asked by the owner of a house to enter through an open door, those facts would clearly not satisfy the category of "breaking in."

In some instances, however, it will not be clear if the facts of a case satisfy or fail to satisfy a legal category. A **legal issue** arises when reasonable people who are knowledgeable about a legal category might disagree about whether the facts of a case or hypothetical satisfy or fail to satisfy a legal category.

The hypothetical case of Gillig and Blasi set out below provides an example of a case in which the facts create **legal issues.**

> Mr. Blasi is a homeless person who spends most nights sleeping in a cardboard structure he made from discarded boxes he found on the street. The structure has two tiny cutouts for windows and a door with a latch on the inside, which is also made from cardboard. The structure is wedged between two posts under a bridge on 11th Street. On the night of February 2 at 10:00 P.M., Mr. Blasi and Mr. Gillig, another homeless man, got into a heated argument under the 11th Street bridge, with Gillig accusing Blasi of stealing his bottle of water. Blasi finally told Gillig: "You're crazy. I never touched your water bottle," and walked away from the argument, retired to his cardboard structure for the night, and latched the door. Gillig was incensed that Blasi had called him crazy and then walked away. Gillig then said to Mr. Schwartz, another homeless person who had been watching the argument: "I am going to slit his throat and then he won't think I'm so crazy." Gillig then pulled a straight razor from his back pocket, went to Blasi's structure, opened the latched door, screamed at Blasi "You won't be calling anyone crazy after I slit your throat," and entered the structure. After Gillig had walked through the door, Schwartz grabbed Gillig from behind and pulled him back into the street. At that time a police car drove up, Schwartz told the police what had happened, and Gillig was arrested and eventually charged with burglary.

Recall that the legal rule defining a burglary is as follows: Burglary is the breaking (Category 1) and entering into (Category 2) the dwelling (Category 3) of another person (Category 4) in the nighttime (Category 5) with the intent to commit a felony (Category 6) therein (Category 7).

The facts of this hypothetical arguably fail to satisfy Category 3 "dwelling," because reasonable people with knowledge of the categories in the burglary rule might disagree about whether the cardboard structure in this case is a "dwelling." Therefore, one **issue** in this hypothetical is whether the cardboard structure is a "dwelling."

The facts of this hypothetical also arguably fail to satisfy Category 1 "breaking," because reasonable people with knowledge of the categories in the burglary rule might disagree about whether entering the structure by opening a cardboard latch without permission would constitute a "breaking." Therefore, a second **issue** in this hypothetical is whether overcoming a cardboard latch constitutes a "breaking."

III. ISSUE SPOTTING

In the classroom and on exams, you will routinely be required to "spot" the issue or issues created by a set of facts. To spot issues, you need to

1. Know the legal rule(s) that apply to a set of facts.

2. Be able to break those rules down into categories.

3. Identify where reasonable people might disagree about whether the facts satisfy or fail to satisfy a legal category.

IV. LAWYERS MAKE ARGUMENTS TO RESOLVE ISSUES

In our legal system, lawyers routinely make arguments to try and convince judges, jurors, and other officials responsible for enforcing the law (e.g., local government officials) to resolve issues in their client's favor. In the *Gillig v. Blasi* burglary case above, for example, assume that Mr. Gillig is charged with burglary and held for trial. At some point before trial, Gillig's attorney will probably ask the trial judge to dismiss the burglary charge against Gillig. Such a request would probably be based on the claim that even if the prosecutor proves all the facts in this case beyond a reasonable doubt, Gillig cannot be convicted of burglary because these facts fail to satisfy the legal categories of "breaking" and "dwelling" in the burglary rule.

The trial judge would then schedule a hearing to rule on the defense's claim that the burglary charge should be dismissed. At this hearing, counsel for the defense and the prosecution will both have an opportunity to make arguments (orally and in writing) about the issues of whether the facts satisfy the categories "dwelling" and "breaking." The trial judge will listen to these arguments, and perhaps construct arguments on his/her own, and then rule on the issue. If the trial judge decides that the facts fail to satisfy one or both of the legal categories, the burglary charge will be dismissed.

Assume, however, that in this case the trial judge decides that the facts of the Gillig case, if proven to a jury beyond a reasonable doubt, would satisfy both legal categories. The case proceeds to trial and Gillig is convicted of burglary. Gillig and his attorney can then appeal to the appellate court and reassert the same claim they made at the trial court. The appellate court then again hears arguments from both the prosecution and the defense about why the facts should either satisfy or fail to satisfy the legal categories "dwelling" and "breaking." After listening to these arguments, the appellate court renders a written opinion, which usually articulates the arguments relied on by the court to resolve these two issues. Although courts may construct arguments of their own to justify their decisions, the arguments courts rely on are frequently those made by the lawyer for a prevailing party.

V. ALL LAWYERS NEED TO BE ABLE TO SPOT ISSUES AND UNDERSTAND THE ARGUMENTS BOTH SIDES MIGHT MAKE TO RESOLVE THEM

When you graduate from law school, you may become a litigator, that is, a lawyer who frequently represents clients seeking to resolve disputes in court or in alternative dispute resolution settings outside the courtroom (e.g., arbitrations). If you engage in this sort of practice, you will obviously need to know how to make arguments resolving issues when you appear before a judge, jury, or an arbitrator. Even if you are a litigator who does not appear in court or before an arbitrator, you will need to imagine and evaluate the persuasiveness of the arguments that will likely be made by both parties to resolve issues. Imagining and evaluating such arguments will help you counsel a client about, among other things, whether to file a case or make or accept a settlement offer.[4]

Even if you have no interest in a litigation practice, you will still need to be able to imagine and evaluate arguments relating to legal issues. In virtually any type of legal practice (e.g., corporate, intellectual property, contracts, etc.) you will encounter legal rules. These rules will all have one or more legal categories, and what your clients want to do in the future (or have done in the past) potentially may create legal issues. You

---

4. Although imagining and evaluating arguments will help you counsel clients, client counseling requires a complicated skill set that goes far beyond imagining and evaluating arguments. See Binder, Bergman, Tremblay & Price, *Lawyers as Counselors* (2d ed., West 2004).

will need to be able to recognize potential issues and counsel your client about the risks created by the issues and the costs and benefits of the alternatives for avoiding or mitigating the risks created by them. In short, learning how to make, imagine, and evaluate arguments relating to legal issues will make you a better problem solver and counselor in all types of legal practice.

Finally, in the short term, you need to know how to recognize issues and make arguments resolving them on many law school exams. Many law school exam questions present you with a set of facts and require you to apply the appropriate legal rules to those facts. To perform well on such questions, you frequently must be able to break legal rules into categories, spot issues, and **make arguments "both ways,"** that is, make arguments that the legal category has been satisfied and arguments that the legal category has not been satisfied.[5]

For example, assume that a question in a criminal law examination provided you with the facts of the *Gillig v. Blasi* case discussed above and asked you to discuss Gillig's liability for burglary. If your answer did nothing more than state the correct rule for burglary and conclude that Gillig <u>could not</u> be convicted of burglary, you would receive a relatively poor grade on the question. This would be true even if the professor <u>agreed</u> with your conclusion.

Now assume that in your answer you correctly state the legal rule for burglary, correctly spot the issues relating to "dwelling" and "breaking," and also make succinct and elegant arguments for both the prosecution and the defense about how to resolve the issues. Your answer concludes by opining that Gillig should not be convicted of burglary. You would receive a high grade for your answer, even if the professor <u>disagreed</u> with your conclusion that Gillig could not be convicted of burglary.

In short, on many law school examinations, spotting issues and crafting tight arguments both ways counts much more than a correct conclusion regarding the ultimate result of the application of a legal rule.

The next chapter provides you with multiple opportunities to practice issue spotting. Chapter 4 then examines several of the arguments commonly used by lawyers and courts to resolve issues.

---

5. For an explanation of why you need to be able to make arguments **both ways**, see Chapter 7.

chapter 3

Issue Spotting in a Rule Application Case — Illustrative Examples

I. INTRODUCTION

As explained in Chapter 2, one of the most basic skills you need to learn in your first year is how to break legal rules into categories and spot issues. Using illustrative examples based on court opinions in subject areas you will study in your first year, this chapter gives you three opportunities to practice this basic skill.

II. ILLUSTRATIVE EXAMPLE #1 — DAISIES AND A TWO-FOOT WALL

A. The Facts

Twenty years ago, Victor Vacant became the owner of Lot 16 in the City of Glendale, when he received a deed to the Lot after he purchased it from the city. At that time, Lot 16 was an empty piece of real estate. After he purchased Lot 16, Vacant did nothing with it. Two years after Vacant purchased Lot 16, John Hope, who owned a house in the city near Lot 16, entered Lot 16 and built a two-foot-high block wall around all but six feet of the 150-foot perimeter of Lot 16. After building the wall, Hope immediately planted a large bed of daisies on the property and twice each year since planting the daisies, Hope entered Lot 16 to cut flowers growing in the daisy bed. To enter and leave Lot 16 for the purpose of cutting flowers, Hope drove his truck through the six-foot opening he had left in the block wall. Hope made no other use of the property on Lot 16.

Hope has now filed a lawsuit against Vacant seeking a court order declaring that Hope has become the legal owner of Lot 16 in the City of Glendale.

B. The Legal Rule

Assume that a legal rule in the State of Uncertainty[1] provides the following: A person who has never received a deed to a parcel of land can be declared the actual owner of the land if the person seeking to become the owner has for at least 15 years either engaged in usual cultivation on the land or protected the land with a substantial enclosure.

C. The Categories in the Legal Rule

Break down the legal rule above into categories. After you have done so, you can compare your breakdown to the one set out below. Before looking at the breakdown below, however, recognize that reasonable people can often disagree about the particular categories into which a rule should be divided. Consequently, your categorical breakdown may not match perfectly the one set out below.

> A person who has never received a deed to a parcel of land can be declared the actual owner of the land: (Category 1)
>
> *If*
>
> the person has for at least 15 years (Category 2)
> engaged in usual cultivation on the land (Category 3)
>
> *or*
>
> *If*
>
> the person has for at least 15 years (Category 4)
> protected the land (Category 5)
> with an enclosure (Category 6)
> which is substantial (Category 7)

---

1. Each of the examples in this chapter is set in the fictional State of Uncertainty. These examples are set in this fictional jurisdiction because this chapter is not intended to teach you the legal rules of any particular state.

D. A Category-by-Category Analysis — Spotting the Issues

Recall that a **legal issue** arises when people knowledgeable about a legal category might reasonably disagree about whether the facts of a case satisfy or fail to satisfy that legal category. To spot the issues in the Hope case, you need to proceed category by category and identify any categories where reasonable people might disagree about whether the facts satisfy the category.

After you have completed your category by category analysis, compare it to the analysis below. Before looking at the analysis below, however, recognize that reasonable people can often disagree about what constitutes an issue. Consequently, the issues you spot may not match perfectly to the issues identified below.

Hope has never received a deed to Lot 16, so the facts of the case clearly satisfy Category 1 **"person who has never received a deed to a parcel of land can be declared the actual owner of the land."** The facts also clearly establish that Hope planted daisies over **15 years** ago and picked daisies twice each year on the land for more than **15 years**, so Category 2 is clearly satisfied.

Reasonable people might disagree, however, about whether Hope's planting and picking daisies satisfies the **"engaged in usual cultivation on the land"** required by Category 3. So one of the issues in this case is whether a single planting of daisies, coupled with picking them twice each year, satisfies "usual cultivation" on the land.

The facts clearly establish that Hope built the block wall more than 15 years ago, so Category 4 is satisfied. Reasonable people might disagree, however, about whether a two-foot-high block wall with a six-foot opening **"protects the land"** as required by Category 5. Similarly, reasonable people might disagree about whether a two-foot-high wall that encircles 144 feet out of 150 feet of the property satisfies the **"enclosure"** requirement of Category 6, and if the wall is an **"enclosure,"** does it satisfy the **"substantial"** requirement of Category 7. Thus, these three categories (**"protects the land,"** **"enclosure,"** and **"substantial"**) each present separate issues under the facts of this case.

III. ILLUSTRATIVE EXAMPLE #2 —
TOWING THE PINTO

A. The Facts

Ashley Clement lived in a residential hotel in the City of Glendale and, with the hotel's permission, parked her Ford Pinto in the hotel's parking lot. The car had not been driven in seven years and Clement did not keep the car's registration current.

Officer Krista Duffy, on a routine patrol for the City of Glendale, noticed an expired registration sticker on Clement's car in the hotel parking lot. Duffy "ran the plates" on Clement's car and learned that Clement had filed a "planned non-operation certificate" with the state department of motor vehicles. This certificate allowed Clement to avoid paying for registration and insurance so long as she did not drive on public roads or park in publicly accessible parking lots.

Without giving notice to Clement or placing a parking ticket on the car, Officer Duffy had Clement's car towed and impounded. Subsequently Clement sued Duffy and the City of Glendale for seizing her Pinto in violation of the state constitution.

B. The Legal Rules

Assume that the constitution of the State of Uncertainty provides that no city or its agent may deprive any person of life, liberty, or property without due process of law. Courts in the State of Uncertainty have interpreted due process of law in this constitutional provision to require that notice must be given to a property owner before seizing property; they also, however, have recognized an exception to the due process requirement that notice be given. Notice need not be given to an owner in an emergency or when a property owner's interest is small relative to the burden that giving notice would impose on the city or its agent.

C. The Categories in the Legal Rules

Again, break down the legal rules above into categories. After you have done so, you can compare your breakdown to the one set out in the box below.

Rule #1

No **city or its agent** (Category 1)
may **deprive** (Category 2)
any **person** (Category 3)
of **life, liberty, or property** (Category 4)
without **due process of law** (Category 5)

Rule #2 (defining Category 5 above)

Due process of law requires that **notice must be given**
  (Category 6)
to a property owner (Category 7)
before seizing property (Category 8)

Rule #3 (providing an exception to the requirement of due
  process)

Due process is not required when the seizure is either **in an
  emergency** (Category 9)

or

the **property owner's interest is small relative to the
  burden that giving notice would impose on the city**
  (Category 10)

D. A Category-by-Category Analysis — Spotting the Issues

To spot the issues, you again need to proceed category by category and identify any categories where reasonable people might disagree about whether the facts satisfy or fail to satisfy the category. After you have completed your category-by-category analysis, compare it to the analysis below.

The facts of the Clement case seem to clearly satisfy some of the legal categories in Rule #1: Glendale is clearly a **"city"** and the police officer is an **"agent"** of the city, so Category 1 is satisfied. Clement is a **"person,"** and her car is **"property,"** so Categories 3 and 4 are clearly satisfied.

Some people might conclude the towing and impounding of Clement's car clearly satisfies Category 2, **"deprived,"** because Clement was prevented from using her car for storage or any other purpose.

Other people might see an issue created with respect to Category 2. The impoundment arguably did not **"deprive"** Clement of her car because she apparently had no intention of driving the car at the time it was impounded.

Category 5, **"without due process of law,"** is defined by Rule #2. Therefore, to determine if Category 5 is satisfied, *each legal category in Rule #2 defining due process of law must be considered separately.* In Clement's case, no notice was given to her before the car was seized so the facts of the case *fail to satisfy* Category 6, **"notice,"** Category 7, **"to the property owner,"** and Category 8, **"before the property is seized."** Therefore, there are no issues with respect to these categories.

Assuming that the seizure of the Pinto deprived Clement of her property without due process of law under Rules #1 and #2, the city can still avoid liability to Clement if the due process exception in Rule #3 applies. The facts clearly fail to satisfy the **"emergency"** category in the Rule #3, because no facts indicate a necessity for immediate seizure of the car. Reasonable people might disagree, however, about whether the facts satisfy or fail to satisfy Category 10, **"property owner's interest is small relative to the burden that giving notice would impose on the city."** Clement clearly has <u>some</u> interest in the seized car because she owns it and has taken the trouble to file a certificate of planned non-operation with the department of motor vehicles. Because Clement was not present when Duffy observed Clement's car, providing notice to Clement before towing the vehicle would entail <u>some</u> burden on the city. But reasonable people might differ about whether Clement's interest is small relative to the city's burden. Therefore, an issue in this case is whether Clement's interest in her car is small relative to the burden that giving notice would impose on the City of Glendale.

IV. ILLUSTRATIVE EXAMPLE #3 — THE POLICE LIEUTENANT'S PROMISE

A. The Facts

Joseph and Eleanor Victum owned a home in the City of Glendale. The home consisted of an apartment on the first floor and an apartment on the second floor. Joseph and Eleanor occupied the second floor apartment. Bart and Barbara Bruiser leased the ground floor apartment from the Victums.

During the first few months of the lease, there were arguments and confrontations between the Victums and the Bruisers, which the police had been called to mediate, and on one occasion in April the Victums filed a formal criminal complaint against the Bruisers. On the night of

July 27, Bart Bruiser physically attacked Eleanor Victum, tearing her blouse and bruising her eye. Eleanor Victum called the Glendale police to complain and Officer Doolittle came to the scene to investigate. Officer Doolittle concluded that the incident was merely a matter of a dispute between landlord and tenant and therefore decided not to make an arrest. After Officer Doolittle left, Joseph Victum arrived home from work and his wife told him what had happened.

Joseph Victum then went to the local police precinct to ask for protection for his family. Joseph spoke with Lieutenant Willing, the desk officer, and told him of the history of confrontations between his family and the Bruisers and that the Bruisers had threatened his wife's safety. Joseph specifically told Willing that he was so concerned that he intended to move his family out of the upper floor apartment of his own house immediately if an arrest was not made. Lieutenant Willing told Joseph that he should not worry and that an arrest would be made or something else would be done about the situation the "first thing tomorrow morning." Joseph then went back to his wife and told her what Lieutenant Willing had said and then Eleanor agreed to unpack her bags and remain in the house.

Despite Lieutenant Willing's assurances, the police did not undertake any further action in response to Joseph's complaint to Willing. At approximately 7:00 P.M. on July 28, the Victums' son Ralston, who did not live with his parents, came to their house for a visit. Immediately after Ralston got out of his car, Bart Bruiser accosted him and the two men had an altercation, which culminated in Ralston's being struck with a baseball bat. Eleanor Victum, who observed the altercation from her upstairs window, and another son, Cyril, rushed to Ralston's rescue. Barbara Bruiser then joined in the attack, slashing at both Eleanor and Cyril with a knife. Eleanor Victum sustained severe personal injuries, and sued the City of Glendale to recover damages for her injuries.

B. The Legal Rule

Assume that in the State of Uncertainty, to prevail in their case, the Victums had to establish a special relationship with the City of Glendale. This special relationship requires the following: an assumption by the city, through promises or actions, of an affirmative duty to act on behalf of the party who was injured; knowledge on the part of the city's agents that inaction could lead to harm; some form of direct contact between the city's agents and the injured party; the injured party's justifiable reliance on the city's assumption of an affirmative duty to act; and that the injury was caused by the injured party's justifiable reliance.

C. The Categories in the Legal Rule

Break down the legal rule above into categories. After you have done so, you can compare your breakdown to the one set out in the box below.

> The legal rule defining a **special relationship** requires that each of the following legal categories be satisfied:
>
> There is an **assumption by the city, through promises or actions, of an affirmative duty to act** (Category 1)
> **on behalf of the party who was injured** (Category 2)
> the **city or its agent knew that inaction could lead to harm** (Category 3)
> there was **direct contact between the city's agents and the injured party** (Category 4)
> the **injured party relied on the city's assumption of an affirmative duty to act** (Category 5)
> the injured party's reliance on the city's assumption of an affirmative duty to act was **reasonable** (Category 6)
> the injured party's reasonable reliance on the city's assumption of an affirmative duty to act was the **cause of the injury** (Category 7)

D. A Category-by-Category Analysis — Spotting the Issues

You know the drill. Proceed category by category and spot the issues in this case. After you have completed your analysis, compare it to the analysis below.

Lieutenant Willing's promise that something would be done about the situation the "first thing tomorrow morning" probably satisfies Category 1, **"assumption by the city, through promises or actions, of an affirmative duty to act."**

The facts of this case also probably satisfy Category 2, **"on behalf of the party who was injured,"** because Joseph Victum requested protection for his family and Willing promised to provide it.

Finally, the facts of this case probably satisfy Category 3, **"the city or its agent knew that inaction could lead to harm,"** because Joseph Victum told Willing of the history of confrontations between his family and the Bruisers and that the Bruisers had threatened his wife's safety.[2]

2. Remember that reasonable people can often disagree about what constitutes an issue. The authors think that Categories 1–3 have been satisfied under the facts of this case, but other reasonable professors or lawyers might disagree.

The injured party, Eleanor Victum, did <u>not</u> speak to Lieutenant Willing. So one issue in this case is whether Joseph's direct contact with Willing, and Joseph's request for protection for his family, satisfies Category 4, **"direct contact between the city's agents and the injured party."**

There is also an issue with respect to Category 5, **"the injured party relied on the city's assumption of an affirmative duty to act."** Willing had promised to do something "first thing in the morning," but Eleanor remained in her apartment until 7:00 P.M. on July 28. Consequently, people might reasonably disagree about whether she stayed until the evening of the 28th in reliance on the promise to take action "in the morning."

Even assuming that Eleanor stayed in the apartment until the evening of the 28th in reliance on Willing's promise, people might reasonably disagree about whether her reliance was reasonable because the police failed to appear in the morning as promised. Thus, there is an issue with respect to Category 6, **"the injured party's reliance on the city's assumption of an affirmative duty to act was reasonable."**

Assuming Eleanor stayed in the apartment until 7:00 P.M. on the evening of July 28 in reliance on Lieutenant Willing's promise, and assuming that her reliance was reasonable, then the facts of this case would seem to clearly satisfy Category 7, "the injured party's reasonable reliance on the city's assumption of an affirmative duty to act was **the cause of the injury**." If Eleanor had not stayed in the apartment until the evening of the 28th she would not have been injured.

V. CONCLUSION: ISSUE SPOTTING REQUIRES EFFORT AND PRACTICE

Breaking legal rules into categories can be a complicated task. Legal rules are usually set forth as "one piece," which tends to obscure the discrete categories in the rule. For example, the rule in the "daisy" case provides that "A person who has never received a deed to a parcel of land can be declared the actual owner of the land if the person seeking to become the owner has for at least 15 years either engaged in usual cultivation on the land or protected the land with a substantial enclosure." When reading this rule, each of the seven categories in the rule may not appear in sharp relief.

In addition, one category in a legal rule is sometimes defined by another legal rule with yet additional categories. For example, in the "towing the Pinto" case the category "without due process of law" is defined by a second legal rule providing that "due process of law requires that notice must be given to a property owner before seizing property."

This definitional relationship may not be obvious to you when you first read a set of legal rules.

Spotting issues can also be difficult because when you begin law school, you may not know if reasonable people with knowledge of a legal category could disagree about whether the facts of a case satisfy or fail to satisfy that legal category. For example, you may not yet have reliable intuitions about what facts satisfy or fail to satisfy a category, such as **"property owner's interest is small relative to the burden that giving notice would impose on the city."** As a result, it is difficult for you to know whether the facts of a case create an issue with respect to that category.

With sustained effort you should improve your issue-spotting skills, as you are repeatedly required to engage in issue spotting when you read court opinions in preparation for class and listen to and participate in classroom dialogues.

Once you have spotted an issue you will frequently be required, either in the classroom or on exams, to argue both ways, that is, to argue that the facts satisfy the legal category and to argue that the facts fail to satisfy the legal category. In the following chapter we discuss some of the arguments typically relied on by courts, lawyers, and law students to argue each side of an issue.

chapter 4

Six Types of Legal Arguments Commonly Used in Rule Application Cases

Your professors will routinely ask you to make "arguments" on behalf of one or both parties to resolve an issue in a rule application case, but your professors may not tell you exactly what constitutes an argument. To help you understand how to make arguments, this chapter illustrates six of the most common types frequently relied on by lawyers and courts to resolve issues. These six types are (1) goal arguments, (2) consequences arguments, (3) principle arguments, (4) arguments by analogy, (5) arguments from precedent, and (6) inference arguments.

Lawyers seldom rely on a single argument when making arguments to a court about how to resolve an issue. Instead, lawyers frequently set forth multiple arguments to resolve a single issue. Thus, for example, a lawyer might use one goal argument, two principle arguments, and one argument from precedent when arguing to a court about a single issue.

Bright lines do not always separate these six types of arguments. Consequently, what you might reasonably see as a principle argument might reasonably be seen by someone else as a goal argument. Also, at times you might have difficulty distinguishing between an argument by analogy and an argument from precedent.

Each of the six types of arguments routinely appears in the opinions you read in all of your first-year courses. Consequently, understanding these argument types will help you to see that you are learning to make the same types of arguments in all of your first-year courses.

This chapter briefly describes and illustrates each of the six types of arguments in isolation and in their simplest and most prototypical form. You should think of these prototypes as analogous to the primary colors red, yellow, and blue. As you will see when you read opinions and make arguments in law school, the six types of arguments can be combined and mixed together to produce many shades of arguments.[1]

---

1. We discuss some of the most common combinations in Chapter 14.

I. GOAL ARGUMENTS

A. What Is a Goal Argument?

Congress, state legislatures, courts, and administrative agencies typically create a legal rule or a body of legal rules to try to accomplish one or more goals. These goals are sometimes referred to as the policies or purposes behind a rule or a body of rules. A goal argument explains why resolving an issue in favor of one party is either consistent or inconsistent with one or more of these goals. To illustrate a goal argument, consider the following two examples.

Assume that the legislature in the State of Confusion passes the following statute: "The use of vehicles is prohibited in public parks. Any person who uses a vehicle in a public park is guilty of a misdemeanor." Alyssa Clement is riding her bicycle through a public park and is cited for violating this statute.[2] You represent Alyssa. You realize that the facts of this case create an issue as to whether a bicycle satisfies or fails to satisfy the legal category "vehicle," because reasonable people could disagree about whether a bicycle is a vehicle. You research the discussions, debates, and reports the legislators had when considering this statute, which is usually called the "legislative history" of the statute. In the legislative history you see the following statement: "This statute is intended to provide a quiet environment in which the public may enjoy the beauty of this State's parks." When Alyssa's case comes up for trial, one of the arguments you make to the judge is the following:

> Your Honor, my client admits that she was riding her bicycle in a public park. However, a bicycle should not be considered a vehicle within the meaning of the statute in this case. As the papers I filed with the court last week indicate, the legislature's goal when passing this statute was to provide a quiet environment in state parks. Given this goal of the legislature, a bicycle should not be considered a vehicle because bicycles typically make almost no noise, and there is no contention that my client's bicycle was making any unusual noise in this case. Therefore a finding that a bicycle is not a vehicle will be consistent with the legislative policy behind this rule.

You have made a goal argument: You have stated the goal behind the statute and explained why deciding that a bicycle fails to satisfy the category "vehicle" will be consistent with the goal of providing quiet enjoyment in the park. Your explanation is contained in the statement "a bicycle should not be considered a vehicle <u>because</u> bicycles typically

---

2. The "no vehicles in the park" hypothetical statute first appeared in H.L.A. Hart, "Positivism and the Separation of Law and Morals," 71 Harv. L. Rev. 593, 606-615 (1958).

make almost no noise and there is no contention that my client's bicycle was making any unusual noise in this case."

Now assume that after representing Alyssa you move to the State of Disarray and become a district attorney. The legislature in the State of Disarray has also passed a statute prohibiting the use of vehicles in the park, and that statute has the exact same language as the one in Alyssa's case.

Your first assignment as district attorney in Disarray is to try the case of Christopher Dylan. Dylan was cited for riding his bicycle through a public park in the State of Disarray. Dylan's attorney has filed papers with the court indicating that the case should be dismissed because a bicycle is not a vehicle within the meaning of statute. You research the legislative history of the statute and find the following statement: "This statute is intended to provide a safe environment for pedestrians using this State's parks." Based on this legislative history, as prosecutor you make the following argument that a bicycle satisfies the legal category "vehicle."

> Your Honor, there is no dispute that the Defendant was riding his bicycle through a public park. Counsel for the defense asserts that a bicycle is not a "vehicle" for purposes of applying the statute at issue in this case. However, the papers I filed with the court last week indicate that the legislative goal when passing this statute was to provide a safe environment for pedestrians using this State's parks. Given this goal of the legislature, a bicycle should be considered a vehicle because pedestrians in the park can easily be injured when struck by a bicycle. Therefore, a finding that a bicycle is a vehicle will be consistent with the legislative policy behind this rule.

Once again, you have made a goal argument: You have stated a goal behind the statute and explained why finding that a bicycle satisfies the category "vehicle" will be consistent with the goal of providing a safe environment for the public ("a bicycle should be considered a vehicle because pedestrians in the park can easily be injured when struck by a bicycle").

B. Arguing Both Ways — Each Party Can Often Use Goal Arguments on the Same Issue

Because there are often multiple and somewhat conflicting goals or policies behind a single legal rule or a body of legal rules, goal arguments **for the same issue** can "point both ways," that is, such arguments can support a finding that the facts satisfy and fail to satisfy a legal category. For example, assume that in a "no vehicles in the park" statute, the legislative history indicates that the legislature wanted to provide a quiet <u>and</u> a safe environment. The attorney for a defendant/bicycle rider cited under such a statute could argue that a goal of the statute is to provide quiet enjoyment, and therefore a bicycle should not be considered a "vehicle." In the same case, the prosecutor could argue that a goal of the statute is to protect pedestrians from injury, and therefore a bicycle should be considered a "vehicle."[3]

II. CONSEQUENCES ARGUMENTS

A. What Is a Consequences Argument?

A goal argument explains that one consequence of resolving an issue may be to further or frustrate a goal motivating the creation of the legal rule(s) containing the legal category creating the issue. Frequently, however, resolving an issue has consequences in the future <u>in addition to</u> furthering or frustrating one or more goals behind a rule. A consequences argument relies on these "beyond the goal" consequences.

When you make a consequences argument, you explain why resolving an issue in favor of one party is likely to minimize or avoid potential negative consequences (either in the short or long term) or likely to encourage or maximize potential positive consequences (either in the short or long term). To illustrate a consequences argument, consider the following examples.

Assume that you now live in the State of Equipoise. The legislature in Equipoise has passed the following, now familiar, statute: "The use of vehicles is prohibited in public parks. Any person who uses a vehicle in a public park is guilty of a misdemeanor." The legislative history of this statute says: "The goal of this statute is to provide a safe environment for pedestrians using this State's parks." Devon Carbado was riding his bicycle through a public park and was cited for violating this statute. You represent Carbado. When Carbado's case comes up for trial, one of the arguments you make to the judge is the following:

> A finding that a bicycle is not a vehicle will encourage the public to use bicycles as transportation. If people are able to ride through parks on their bicycles to get to work or to shop for groceries, then they will be less likely to drive their car to work or when running errands. Less auto traffic will produce less congestion and less pollution.

This is a consequences argument because it explains why a decision that a bicycle is not a vehicle might produce the positive consequences of reducing congestion and pollution.

---

3. For a further discussion of "goal arguments," see Chapter 14.

Consider another example of a consequences argument. Assume that the highest court in the State of Equipoise announces the following legal rule: "When an employee has been employed for a substantial period of time by one employer, that employee may be terminated from employment by that employer only for good cause. An employee who has not been employed for a substantial period of time may be terminated for any reason." The court also states its purpose for announcing this rule is to provide a uniform standard that will apply to all employment termination cases in the State of Equipoise.

Cambra Jones was employed by the Soft Software Co. ("Soft") for two months as a programmer and then terminated. Cambra contends she performed extremely well as a programmer and that she was terminated because she had a personal disagreement with one of her supervisors outside of work. Cambra sues Soft for allegedly terminating her without "good cause."

You represent Soft, and you recognize that Cambra's two-month period of employment may satisfy or fail to satisfy the legal category "substantial period of time" in the above rule. You file papers with the court contending that Cambra cannot sue Soft because she was not employed by Soft for a "substantial period of time." Therefore, Soft can terminate Cambra for any reason. When you appear before the Judge, one of the arguments you make is the following:

> Your Honor, both parties agree that Ms. Jones was only employed by Soft for two months. That period should not be considered a "substantial period of time." If two months is a substantial period of time, a huge number of employees will be able to claim that they were terminated without good cause and lawsuits by terminated employees will overwhelm the courts of this State. In addition, a finding that two months is a substantial period of time will hurt employees. An employee may need more that two months to demonstrate to an employer that they are a valuable addition to the employer's enterprise. This is especially likely where the employee must develop the job specific skills that are required for many high-paying, skilled jobs. But if an employer knows that they can be subject to suit for terminating an employee after two months, the employer will have an incentive not to take a chance on an employee who is less than perfect at the end of two months. As a result, there will be more employee turnover and more unemployment insurance claims if two months is found to be a "substantial period of time."

This is a consequences argument because it explains why a finding that two months fails to satisfy the legal category "substantial period of time" might avoid negative consequences, namely, flooding the courts with lawsuits relating to employment termination and increasing employee turnover.

B. Arguing Both Ways — Each Party Can Often Use Consequences Arguments on the Same Issue

The resolution of an issue routinely results in what might reasonably be seen as both positive and negative consequences. As a result, opposing parties can both make consequences arguments **for the same issue**. For example, in the employee termination case above, a lawyer for an employer may argue that ruling that two months <u>is</u> a substantial period of time may result in many lawsuits by terminated employees that will burden the court system, which is a negative consequence, and that consequence may be avoided or mitigated by a ruling that two months is not a substantial period of time. But a lawyer for an employee can also argue that a ruling that two months <u>is not</u> a substantial period will create negative consequences. For example, such a ruling would encourage employers to terminate short-term employees for arbitrary reasons. Therefore, the court should mitigate or minimize that negative consequence with a ruling that two months is a substantial period of time.

III. PRINCIPLE ARGUMENTS

A. What Is a Principle Argument?

Principles are generally accepted normative guidelines suggesting how people should behave, how documents or texts should be interpreted, and how events should usually happen. Think of principles as similar to legal rules, but softer and less controlling of the outcome in a legal dispute. A principle argument explains why resolving an issue is consistent with one or more principles. To illustrate a principle argument, consider the following examples.

Assume that you are now the prosecutor in the State of Equipoise. Recall that the legislature in Equipoise has passed the now familiar statute: "The use of vehicles is prohibited in public parks. Any person who uses a vehicle in a public park is guilty of a misdemeanor." You are prosecuting Mike Schill, who was riding his bicycle through a public park and was cited for violating this statute. When Schill's case comes up for trial, one of the arguments you make to the judge is the following:

> Your Honor, it is a generally accepted principle that words in legal rules are usually to be given their ordinary meaning. Webster's dictionary defines a vehicle as "a means of transporting something. . . ." A bicycle can be used to transport people or things and therefore a finding that a bicycle is a vehicle will be consistent with the principle of giving words in legal rules their ordinary meaning.

You have made a principle argument: You have articulated a principle, namely, words in legal rules should usually be given their ordinary meaning,[4] and you have explained why a finding that a bicycle satisfies the legal category "vehicle" would be consistent with this principle.

Consider another example. Harold and Winona have been married for ten years and have two children, ages 7 and 9. Harold is a real estate developer who is about to undertake a major real estate development, which he anticipates will be very profitable in several years. Harold decides that he does not want his wife to share in the anticipated profits from the real estate development. Therefore, Harold goes to Winona and says: "I want you to sign an agreement accepting $500,000 as a complete settlement of all your claims against me in the event we should divorce in the future. If you do not agree to sign the agreement I will immediately initiate divorce proceedings." At the time Harold proposes this agreement, Harold and Winona's marital property is worth $2 million.

Winona consults a lawyer, who advises her that she should not sign the agreement because she will receive $1 million (one-half of the marital property) if Harold divorces her now and if she signs the agreement it will probably be enforceable and limit her to $500,000 in the event of any future divorce. Despite her lawyer's advice, Winona decides to sign the agreement because she thinks doing so will encourage Harold to remain in the marriage and she does not want her children to suffer the consequences of a divorce.

Three years later, Harold files for divorce. The real estate development project has been very profitable, and as a result the marital property is now worth $10 million. In the absence of the agreement she signed, Winona would be entitled to $5 million as a result of the divorce. The applicable legal rule provides that the agreement Winona signed is enforceable if it is "fair." You represent Winona. One argument you make to the judge in this case is as follows:

> Your Honor, one party to an existing marriage should not be able to use the threat of a divorce to bargain themselves into a position of advantage. That's what Harold did in this case: He used the threat of divorce to obtain an agreement that allows him to keep more than half of the community estate; therefore, the agreement Winona signed is not fair and should not be enforced.

You have made a principle argument: You have articulated a principle, namely, that one party to an existing marriage should usually not be able to use the threat of the divorce to bargain themselves into a position of advantage. You have also explained why resolving the issue

---

4. One of the most common principle arguments is that words should usually be given their ordinary meaning.

of whether the agreement is "fair" would be consistent with that principle.[5]

B. Arguing Both Ways — Each Party Can Often Use Principle Arguments on the Same Issue

Principles used to resolve issues are typically not absolutes; instead, they are generally accepted statements about how people should <u>usually</u> behave, how texts should <u>usually</u> be interpreted, or how things should <u>usually</u> happen. Consequently, virtually all principles are subject to exceptions, and you can profitably think of virtually all principles as beginning with limiting phrases like "Generally speaking . . ." or "In the majority of cases. . . ." Because principles are typically not absolutes, opposing parties can make principle arguments **for the same issue.**

For instance, in the Harold v. Winona example above, we have examined a principle argument that the agreement signed by Winona is not fair and should not be enforced. But an attorney representing Harold can make a principle argument that the agreement Winona signed is fair, and Harold should prevail. One such principle argument might go as follows:

> Your Honor, when a competent adult signs a contract after being fully advised of her legal rights and the probable consequences of signing the contract, the contract should be enforced. Winona was advised by a lawyer as to consequences of signing the contract in this case, and she knew that she might receive less than half of the marital estate when she signed the contract. Therefore, the contract was fair at the time it was signed and should be enforced.

This argument articulates a principle — when a competent adult signs a contract after being fully advised of her legal rights and the probable consequences of signing the contract, the contract should generally be enforced — and explains why this principle supports a conclusion that the contract Winona signed was "fair."

IV. A WORD ABOUT "POLICY" ARGUMENTS

You may often hear your classmates (and your professors) refer to "policy" arguments in your first year of law school. "Policy" arguments typically include what we refer to as goal arguments, consequences arguments, and principle arguments. We think that separating "policy"

---

5. For a further discussion of "principle arguments," see Chapter 14.

arguments into these three types of arguments provides greater clarity. Resolution of an issue can be "good policy" because it is (1) consistent with a goal behind a rule, (2) consistent with a principle, (3) will produce positive consequences or avoid negative consequences in the future, or (4) will accomplish some combination of (1), (2), and (3).

V. ARGUMENTS BY ANALOGY

A. What Is an Argument by Analogy?

An issue is sometimes **similar to** an issue previously decided by a prior court case or resolved by another respected source (e.g., law reviews, legal treatises, etc.). In its simplest and most prototypical form, an argument by analogy explains why a previously decided issue is similar to an issue currently under consideration and asserts that the issue currently under consideration should be resolved in the same way as the previously decided issue. To illustrate an argument by analogy, consider the following example.

Assume that the legislature in the State of Rigidity has passed the apparently very popular statute providing that: "The use of vehicles is prohibited in public parks. Any person who uses a vehicle in a public park is guilty of a misdemeanor." Eric Zolt is riding his bicycle through a public park and is cited for violating this statute. You represent Zolt. When Zolt's case comes up for trial, among the arguments you make to the judge is the following:

> Your Honor, my client admits that he was riding his bicycle in a public park. However, a bicycle should not be considered a vehicle within the meaning of the statute in this case. In the papers I filed with the court last week, I cited the case of *People v. Zasloff*, which was decided just a year ago by the appellate court in this state. In that case the defendant, Zasloff, was riding his skateboard through a public park and was charged with violating the same statute as is at issue in this case. The appellate court held that Zasloff was not guilty because a skateboard was not a "vehicle" under this statute. A skateboard is similar to a bicycle because the use of both <u>creates a minimum amount of noise</u>, both are used <u>by an individual for transportation</u>, and both <u>pose some risk of injury to pedestrians</u>. Because a skateboard is not a "vehicle" under this statute, this court should rule that a bicycle is not a "vehicle" and dismiss this case.

You have made an argument by analogy: You have established that a previous court decision ruled that a skateboard did not satisfy the legal category "vehicle" under the statute in question. To establish similarity between the previously decided issue and the issue to be decided, you focus on **features** or **attributes** common to both issues. That is, you explain that both a skateboard and a bicycle create a minimum amount of noise, are used by an individual for transportation, and pose some risk of injury to pedestrians. After explaining that the two issues are similar, you ask the court to find that a bicycle is not a "vehicle" under the statute in question.

In your first year, the source of many arguments by analogy will be court opinions. But any respected source may be the basis of an argument by analogy. For example, a law review or legal treatise may contain an opinion that a skateboard should not be considered a vehicle under the "no vehicles in the park" statute. You could use that law review or treatise to make an argument by analogy in a bicycle case.

B. Arguing Both Ways — Each Party Can Often Use Arguments by Analogy on the Same Issue

There are often multiple previously resolved issues by one or more court opinions or other respected sources that are similar to an issue under consideration. One previously resolved similar issue may be consistent with a finding for one party, whereas another previously resolved similar issue will be consistent with a finding for an opposing party. Consequently, opposing parties may both make arguments by analogy **for the same issue.** For example, assume that the prosecutor in the above case against Zolt makes the following argument:

> Your Honor, in the papers I filed with the court last week, I cited the case of *People v. Eagly*, which was decided just a year ago by the appellate court in this State. In that case the defendant, Ingrid Eagly, was riding her bicycle in a school zone on public school property. The court held that Eagly was guilty of a misdemeanor under a Rigidity statute providing that "It is a misdemeanor to use a <u>vehicle</u> in a school zone on public school property." The statute in this case relates to the use of vehicles in the public parks, and the statute in the *Eagly* case related to the use of vehicles in a school zone. These statutes are similar because they both <u>regulate traffic in public spaces frequented by pedestrians</u>. Therefore, because a bicycle is a "vehicle" under the school zone statute, it should also be a "vehicle" in this case.

In this example, the prosecutor has made an argument by analogy indicating that Zolt's bicycle should be considered a vehicle. The prosecutor establishes that a previous court decision held that a bicycle was a vehicle under a **different** statute, explains why the statute at issue in the previous case has similar **features** or **attributes** to the statute at issue in Zolt's case, and asks the court to find that a bicycle is therefore a "vehicle."[6]

VI. ARGUMENTS FROM PRECEDENT

A. What Is an Argument from Precedent?

A prior case or other respected source may have previously decided the exact same issue that is currently under consideration. An argument from precedent explains that the exact same issue has previously been decided and asserts that the result in the previous decision should be controlling. To illustrate an argument from precedent, consider the following example.

Assume that the legislature in the State of Denial has jumped on the bandwagon and passed the following statute: "The use of vehicles is prohibited in public parks. Any person who uses a vehicle in a public park is guilty of a misdemeanor." Lynn Stout is riding her bicycle through a public park and is cited for violating this statute. You represent Stout. When Stout's case comes up for trial, one of the arguments you make to the judge is the following:

> Your Honor, my client admits that she was riding her bicycle in a public park. However, a bicycle should not be considered a vehicle within the meaning of the statute at issue in this case. In the papers I filed with the court last week, I cited the case of *People v. Cummings*, which was decided just a year ago by the appellate court in the State of Uncertainty. In that case the defendant, Cummings, was riding her bicycle through a public park and was charged with violating a statute in the State of Uncertainty with the exact same language as the State of Denial statute at issue in this case. The appellate court in the State of Uncertainty held that Cummings was not guilty because a bicycle was not a "vehicle" under the Uncertainty statute. Your Honor, you should follow the decision of the court in the State of Uncertainty and find that a bicycle is not a "vehicle" under the Denial statute at issue in this case, and dismiss this case.

You have made an argument from precedent: You have established that a previous court decision established that a bicycle was not a "vehicle" under a statute with the same language as the statute involved in your client's case. You then ask the court to follow the decision in the prior case.

6. For a further discussion of "arguments by analogy," see Chapter 14.

B. Arguing Both Ways — Each Party Can Often Use Precedent Arguments on the Same Issue

Often multiple cases or authoritative sources will have previously decided an issue, and not every prior decision will have reached the same conclusion. Consequently, opposing parties can frequently both make arguments from precedent **for the same issue**. For example, assume that the prosecutor in the above case against Stout makes the following argument from precedent:

> Your Honor, in the papers I filed with the court last week, I cited the case of *People v. Rowe*, which was decided just a year ago by the appellate court in the State of Repose. In that case the defendant Rowe was riding his bicycle through a public park and was charged with violating a statute in the State of Repose with the exact same language as the State of Denial statute at issue in this case. The appellate court in the State of Repose held that Rowe was guilty because a bicycle was a "vehicle" under the Repose statute. Your Honor, you should follow the decision of the court in the State of Repose and find that a bicycle is a "vehicle" under the Denial statute at issue in this case.

C. The Special Case of "Binding" or "Controlling" Precedent

Sometimes an argument from precedent can <u>require</u> a court to reach a certain result when resolving an issue. Assume, for example, that the highest court in the State of Grace has held that a bicycle is a "vehicle" under the statute prohibiting the use of vehicles in the park. That decision by the highest court in the State of Grace is binding or controlling precedent for all <u>lower</u> courts in the State of Grace, i.e., the decision <u>must</u> be followed by all the <u>lower</u> courts in the State of Grace (but may or may not be followed by courts in other states).[7]

Exactly what constitutes binding or controlling precedent is a subject that should be covered in detail in at least one of your first-year law school courses.

---

7. When there is binding or controlling precedent, one might say that the precedent mandates a decision regarding an issue. Alternatively, when there is binding or controlling precedent, one might say that there is no issue in the case. Thus, if the highest court in the State of Grace has ruled that a bicycle is a vehicle under the "no vehicles in the park" statute, a second case involving a bicycle in the State of Grace might be seen as not raising an issue about whether a bicycle is a "vehicle" under the statute.

VII. INFERENCE ARGUMENTS

A. What Is an Inference Argument?

An inference is a conclusion of fact drawn from circumstantial evidence. For example, assume that witnesses testify to the following items of circumstantial evidence: One of Bob's parents recently died after a long illness, and after being informed of the death Bob was sitting alone and crying in the kitchen. From this evidence, one can infer (or conclude) that Bob was in fact sad when he was crying in the kitchen.

Courts and juries will frequently draw inferences of fact from circumstantial evidence, especially about the **intent** or other **state of mind** of one or more people, when resolving an issue. In a case involving an alleged breach of contract, for example, a court may be required to draw inferences about the intent of the parties creating the contract to resolve an issue relating to the legal category "breach." And, in a murder case, a court may be required to draw inferences about a defendant's state of mind when addressing an issue relating to the legal category "intent to kill."

In its simplest form, an inference argument marshals the circumstantial evidence of the fact to be inferred. To illustrate an inference argument, consider the following example.

Paula Pickford and Daniel Dolinko are involved in an auto accident. You file suit on behalf of Pickford, alleging that Dolinko was negligent at the time of the accident because he was speeding. Dolinko denies that he was speeding. At the time of the accident, Dolinko had just picked his son up from day care and was proceeding on to a business meeting. At trial, you make the following argument to the jury:

> Mr. Dolinko denies that he was speeding. The judge will instruct you that it is up to you to look at all the evidence and decide whether or not Mr. Dolinko was speeding. Now, Mr. Dolinko's own testimony establishes that at the time of the accident he was late for an important business meeting with Ms. Grady, a prospective new customer for Mr. Dolinko. And he admits that he arranged this meeting with Ms. Grady himself, that Ms. Grady had been reluctant to meet with him in the past, and that he had been unable to call ahead and let Ms. Grady know that he would be late for their meeting. Your common sense will tell you that under these circumstances, Mr. Dolinko was probably exceeding the speed limit in an attempt to get to his meeting with Ms. Grady as soon as possible.

You have made an inference argument. You have marshaled the circumstantial evidence that supports the inference that Mr. Dolinko was speeding at the time of the accident.

B. Arguing Both Ways — Each Party Can Often Use Inference Arguments on the Same Issue

Inferences from circumstantial evidence are based on generalizations about what often or frequently happens. As a result, one can never be absolutely sure that a fact inferred from circumstantial evidence is correct. For example, people who are late to an important meeting may often speed to get there as soon as possible, but that is not always the case. Because inferences from circumstantial evidence are based on generalizations, opposing parties can both make inference arguments regarding **the same issue**. For example, in the *Pickford v. Dolinko* case above, the lawyer for Dolinko could make the following inference argument that Dolinko was <u>not</u> speeding at the time of the accident:

> The Plaintiff contends that my client was speeding to get to a meeting with Ms. Grady. But remember what Mr. Dolinko told you on the stand: He had his two-year-old son in the back seat at the time of this accident and he was driving slowly and cautiously, as he always did when he had his child in the car. And your common sense will tell you that you can believe Mr. Dolinko when he says he was driving below the speed limit because parents **generally** are concerned about their children and don't want to risk an injury to them by speeding.

VIII. NONE OF THE SIX ARGUMENT TYPES IS NECESSARILY DISPOSITIVE

With the exception of arguments based on **binding** precedent, none of the six types of arguments is necessarily dispositive. In other words, there is no fixed persuasive hierarchy among the argument types. Thus, for example, a court might find that your goal, principle, and precedent arguments are sound but still find that your opponent's consequences argument carries greater persuasive force. Alternatively, a court might find that your goal, principle, and precedent arguments carry greater persuasive force than a sound consequences argument by your opponent.[8]

---

8. Chapter 15 addresses the nature of the decision a judge must make to assess the persuasive force of competing arguments.

IX. COURTS RELY ON ONE OR MORE OF THE SIX TYPES OF ARGUMENTS TO JUSTIFY AND EXPLAIN THEIR DECISIONS

After considering the parties' arguments about how to resolve an issue, a court will reach a decision, usually in a written opinion. The opinion will frequently rely on one or more of the six types of arguments to explain or justify its decision with respect to each issue in a case. The arguments relied on by a court are sometimes the same arguments that were made by one of the lawyers in the case (usually the lawyer for the prevailing party). In many cases, however, a court may explain and justify its decision with arguments that were not made by any of the parties. As you will see in the next two chapters, when you read court opinions for class, and are questioned about those opinions in the classroom, you will need to be able to articulate and critique the arguments in the court's opinion. You will be better able to do this if you understand the six different types of arguments discussed in this chapter.

X. WHERE ARGUMENTS COME FROM: THE SOURCES OF THE SIX TYPES OF ARGUMENTS

As discussed earlier in this chapter, court opinions and other legal materials are a common and important source for arguments by analogy and arguments from precedent. Court opinions and other legal materials may also help you make the other legal arguments discussed in this chapter. For example, a court opinion may state the goal behind a legal rule; then you may be able to use that same goal when making a goal argument in another case. Similarly, court opinions or legal treatises may announce principles or consequences that you can add to your argument repertoire, and use in the future to construct arguments.[9]

Court opinions and other legal materials are not, however, the only sources that you can use to construct arguments. You can use respected sources from literature, proverbs, economics, history, philosophy, quantitative methods, legal theories (e.g., law and economics, critical race studies, etc.), and psychology to construct arguments. Consider just a few examples. Quantitative methods, economics, and psychology may help you (or a court) to predict the likely consequences of resolving an issue. Philosophical maxims may support a principle argument. Well-known stories from literature may serve as the source of arguments by analogy.

---

9. Chapter 14 will address in more detail the use of prior cases to construct arguments.

The range of sources used to construct legal arguments may explain, at least in part, why law schools admit students with a broad range of experiences and undergraduate majors. A classmate with ten years experience as a police officer may be better at predicting the likely consequences of resolving issues in legal rules placing limits on police interrogation of suspects than a law student who has little or no experience dealing with the police. A colleague with an undergraduate degree in history may be particularly adept at making arguments by analogy.

In some of your courses, a professor may require you to learn a fair amount about a legal or nonlegal discipline and/or a particular industry through outside assigned readings or research to help you to identify the potential consequence of resolving issues or to learn principles reflected in the norms of a particular culture or industry. For example, in a torts course you may be required to learn a good deal about law and economics and the insurance industry to identify the likely consequences of resolving issues in torts cases.

XI. A WORD ABOUT THE TERM "ARGUMENT"

Although court opinions routinely rely on one or more of the six types of arguments to justify the resolution of an issue, a court opinion frequently will not use the words "argument" or "arguments" to explain the justification for a decision. Thus, for example, court opinions usually do <u>not</u> say something like the following: "The arguments supporting our decision are as follows. . . ." Similarly, your professors may not ask you for the "arguments" supporting a court's decision on an issue. Instead, professors might ask you why the court found as it did, or ask you for a court's "reasoning," "rationale," "explanation for" or "justification for" its resolution of an issue.

We characterize a court's justification for its decision as one or more arguments to emphasize that **when the facts present an issue there are almost always sound and reasonable arguments that would support a decision directly contrary to the one reached in a court opinion.** And, as you will see in Chapter 7, in the classroom professors will sometimes ask you to articulate the arguments that would support such a contrary result.

chapter 5

Reading Rule Application Opinions in Preparation for Class — Preparing a Case "Brief"

I. INTRODUCTION

Prior chapters have discussed and illustrated the concepts of legal rules, legal categories, issues, and legal arguments. Using the opinion in *Bridges v. Diesel*, one that you might be asked to read in your Civil Procedure class, this chapter explores how these concepts can help you create a case "brief" for class when reading an opinion involving rule application. Your case brief is the written preparation you will take into the classroom. At the conclusion of this chapter, we provide you with an illustrative example of a case brief in the *Bridges* case.

II. *BRIDGES V. DIESEL SERVICE, INC.* 1994 U.S. DIST. LEXIS 9429 (E.D. PA. 1994)

A. Background Information

The following background information may help you to understand the court's opinion in *Bridges*.

Under the Americans with Disabilities Act (ADA), a statute passed by Congress, a plaintiff is required to exhaust administrative remedies before filing a lawsuit. Exhausting administrative remedies means that a plaintiff must file a document (called a "charge") with the Equal Employment Opportunity Commission (EEOC) <u>before</u> filing a lawsuit in federal court. If the plaintiff's complaint about the alleged violation of the ADA is not satisfactorily resolved before the EEOC, <u>then</u> a plaintiff may file suit in federal court. In the *Bridges* case, James Bridges filed a lawsuit against defendant Diesel Service, Inc., alleging a violation of the ADA. The plaintiff's lawyer did not, however, file a charge with the EEOC <u>before</u> filing a lawsuit in federal court.

The defendant claimed that plaintiff's counsel's filing of the suit before exhausting administrative remedies by filing a charge with the EEOC was a violation of Rule 11 of the Federal Rules of Civil Procedure (FRCP). The defendant also asked the court for monetary sanctions against the plaintiff's counsel for allegedly violating Rule 11. Therefore, in this opinion the court decides (1) whether plaintiff's counsel's filing of suit before exhausting administrative remedies violated Rule 11 and (2) if there was a violation of Rule 11, whether plaintiff's counsel should be required to pay sanctions to the defendant.

B. The Applicable Provisions of FRCP 11

In civil procedure class, you will frequently be assigned to read the applicable portions of the FRCP at the same time you are assigned to read a case.[1] Thus, if you are assigned the *Bridges* case, you will also probably be asked to read Rule 11 of the FRCP. In pertinent part, Rule 11 reads as follows:

Rule 11. Signing of Pleadings, Motions, and Other Papers; Representations to the Court; Sanctions

(a) . . .

(b) **Representations to the Court.** By presenting to the court . . . a pleading, written motion, or other paper, an attorney . . . is certifying that to the best of the person's knowledge, information and belief, formed after an inquiry reasonable under the circumstances, —

(1) . . .

(2) the claims, defenses, . . . therein are warranted by existing law. . . .

(3) the allegations and other factual contentions have evidentiary support. . . .

(4) . . .

(c) **Sanctions.** If . . . the court determines that subdivision (b) has been violated, the court may . . . impose an appropriate sanction upon the attorneys . . . that have violated subdivision (b) . . .

(2) A sanction imposed for the violation of this rule shall be limited to what is sufficient to deter repetition of such conduct or comparable conduct by others similarly situated . . .

---

1. In your other first-year courses, you may also be assigned to read supplemental materials in conjunction with a court opinion.

C. The Court's Opinion in *Bridges v. Diesel*

James Bridges ("Plaintiff") commenced this action against Diesel Service, Inc. ("Defendant") under the Americans with Disabilities Act ("ADA"), 42 U.S.C. §12101 et seq. By Order dated June 29, 1994, the Court dismissed Plaintiff's Complaint without prejudice for failure to exhaust administrative remedies. In particular, Plaintiff did not file a charge with the Equal Employment Opportunity Commission ("EEOC") until after commencement of this action. Defendant now moves for sanctions pursuant to Fed. R. Civ. P. 11. For the following reasons, Defendant's motion is DENIED.

. . . As explained in this Court's June 29 Order, the filing of a charge with the EEOC is still a condition precedent to maintenance of a discrimination suit under the ADA. . . . The parties do not dispute that administrative remedies must be exhausted before commencement of an action under the ADA. Indeed, Plaintiff's counsel stated that it would stipulate to dismissal of the Complaint without prejudice provided Defendant does not explicitly retain the right to move for sanctions under Fed. R. Civ. P. 11.

Rule 11 "imposes an obligation on counsel and client analogous to the railroad crossing sign, 'Stop, Look and Listen'. It may be rephrased, 'Stop, Think, Investigate and Research' before filing papers either to initiate the suit or to conduct the litigation." . . . Rule 11 is violated only if, at the time of signing, the signing of the document filed was objectively unreasonable under the circumstances. . . . Ford Motor Co. v. Summit Motor Products, Inc., 930 F.2d 277, 289 (3d Cir.), cert. denied, 112 S.Ct. 373 (1991). "[T]he Rule does not permit the use of the 'pure heart and an empty head' defense." Gaiardo, 835 F.2d at 482. Rather, counsel's signature certifies the pleading is supported by a reasonable factual investigation and "a normally competent level of legal research." Lieb v. Topstone Industries, Inc., 788 F.2d 151, 157 (3d Cir. 1986).

The Court is not convinced that Plaintiff's counsel displayed a competent level of legal research. A brief review of case law would have revealed the EEOC filing requirement. Further, an award of sanctions for failure to exhaust administrative remedies is not unprecedented. See, e.g., Worrell v. Uniforms To You & Co., 673 F. Supp. 1461 (N.D. Cal. 1987); Khan v. Loyola Univ. Chicago, No. 91 C 8344, 1992 U.S. Dist LEXIS 15060 (E.D. Pa. 1992).

Notwithstanding, the Court will not grant sanctions. Rule 11 is not intended as a general fee shifting device. Gaiardo, 835 F.2d at 483. The prime goal of Rule 11 sanctions is deterrence of improper conduct. Waltz v. County of Lycoming, 974 F.2d 387, 390 (3d Cir. 1992); Doering v. Union County Bd. of Chosen Freeholders, 857 F.2d 191, 194 (3d Cir. 1988). In this case, monetary sanctions are not necessary to deter future misconduct. Plaintiff's counsel immediately acknowledged its error and attempted to rectify the situation by filing a charge with the EEOC and moving to place this action in civil suspense. In fact, the Complaint has been dismissed without prejudice. The Court expects that Plaintiff's counsel has learned its lesson and will demonstrate greater diligence in future.

Further, Rule 11 sanctions should be reserved for those exceptional circumstances where the claim asserted is patently unmeritorious or frivolous. Doering, 857 F.2d at 194. The mistake in the present case was procedural rather than substantive. . . . Finally, the Court is aware of the need to avoid "chilling" Title VII litigation. . . .

For the above stated reasons, Defendant's motion pursuant to Fed. R. Civ. P. 11 is DENIED. However, this Opinion should not be read as condoning the conduct of Plaintiff's counsel. As stated above, the standard of pre-filing research was below that required of competent counsel. Plaintiff's case has been dismissed without prejudice. If the action is refiled, the Court fully expects to see a high standard of legal product from Plaintiff's counsel — in particular attorney London, who signed the Complaint.

III. PREPARING A CASE BRIEF FOR CLASS IN *BRIDGES V. DIESEL*

As you read an opinion in preparation for class, you will benefit from identifying each of the following and recording them in your case brief:

- The issue or issues in the opinion.
- The arguments relied on by the court to resolve each issue.
- The legal rules relating to the issues in the opinion.
- A summary of the facts in the opinion.

The sections below discuss these four aspects of a case brief in the *Bridges* opinion and explain how identifying them can help you to understand classroom dialogues and discussions, to answer law school exam questions, and to succeed in the practice of law.

A. The First Issue in *Bridges v. Diesel*

In *Bridges*, Plaintiff's attorney filed a complaint without first exhausting administrative remedies by filing a charge with the EEOC. One of the issues the court had to decide was whether these facts satisfy or fail to satisfy the legal category: **"normally competent level of legal research."**

1. The Benefits of Identifying the Issues in Preparation for Class

Identifying the issues in an opinion will help you respond to common questions asked by professors and to understand classroom dialogues between a professor and your colleagues. For example, when discussing *Bridges* in the classroom, a professor is likely to ask a question like, "Ms. Abernathy, with respect to the violation of Rule 11, what was the issue the court in *Bridges* had to decide?" Ms. Abernathy might respond to the professor's question by saying something like, "The court had to decide whether filing a complaint without first filing a charge with the EEOC meant that the complaint was not supported by a normally competent level of legal research."

Learning to identify or spot issues as you read opinions in preparation for class will also help you practice a skill you will frequently need on law school exams and in law practice. In one type of exam question, you will be given a set of facts and will need to spot the issues in the legal rules that apply to those facts.[2] Identifying issues as you read opinions for class will provide you with practice in this critical exam-taking skill. When you read opinions in law practice, you will also need to identify the issue(s) addressed and resolved by the court in its opinion.

2. Difficulties Identifying Issues in an Opinion

In some opinions, identifying the issue will be relatively easy. A court opinion will sometimes do the work for you by explicitly identifying the legal category where the facts create an issue. In *Bridges*, for example, the court might have said something like, "The first issue we must decide in this case is whether filing a complaint without first exhausting administrative remedies by filing a charge with the EEOC constitutes a failure to engage in a normally competent level of legal research, and therefore violates Rule 11."

Frequently, however, opinions will **not** explicitly identify the "issue" or "question" in a case; and, even when the opinion does identify an "issue" or "question," it may use these terms quite broadly. For example, in *Bridges* the court might have said something like, "The issue we must decide is whether filing a complaint without first exhausting administrative remedies violates Rule 11." Such a broad statement of the "issue" does not identify the **specific legal category** which may or may not be satisfied by the facts in the case.

When a court's definition of the issue or question does not clearly identify the **specific legal category** at issue, for several reasons you may have difficulty identifying the issue. (Indeed, when you read the *Bridges* opinion you may not have realized that one of the issues in the opinion involved the legal category "normally competent level of legal research.")

---

2. Identifying or spotting issues is only one of the skills you need to acquire to perform well on law school exams. As you prepare for exams, you may want to review prior law school exams and model answers, talk to your colleagues or professors about exam-taking strategies and approaches, or read books on the subject.

A court opinion frequently contains many legal rules, and the opinion will not highlight in **bold** the precise legal rule containing the legal category at issue. The relatively short opinion in *Bridges*, for example, contains at least the following legal rules:

> The filing of a charge with the EEOC is a condition precedent to maintenance of a discrimination suit under the ADA.

> Rule 11 is violated only if, at the time of signing, the signing of the document filed was objectively unreasonable under the circumstances.

> Counsel's signature certifies that a pleading is supported by a reasonable factual investigation and a normally competent level of legal research.

Especially early on in your law school career, you may have difficulty determining which of these rules contains the legal category that may or may not be satisfied by the facts of the case.

In addition, you may have difficulty identifying an issue because you will often be unfamiliar with some of the words or phrases in the categories in legal rules. For example, you may be unfamiliar with legal terms such as "quasi-contract," "subject matter jurisdiction," "constructive condition," "vested remainder," "covenant running with the land," "equitable estoppel," and "mens rea."[3] Also, many words that you are already familiar with may have a special meaning when used in legal rules. For example, "consideration" does not have the same legal meaning in a breach of contract case that it has in ordinary social conversation. If you are uncertain of the meaning of the words in a legal rule, it may be difficult to break the rule down into legal categories or recognize when the facts may or may not satisfy each category.

3. Tips for Identifying Issues in an Opinion

When you have difficulty identifying an issue, ask yourself one or both of the following questions:

> **What conduct did one or both of the parties, or their representatives, engage in that seemed to concern the court?**

> **What conduct did one or both of the parties, or their representatives, engage in that is emphasized in the opinion?**

Then, try to tie your answers to these questions to a legal category. In the *Bridges* case, for example, the court seems to be concerned with plaintiff's counsel's failure to file a claim with the EEOC. This failure

---

3. If you do not understand a legal term in the opinion, get in the habit of looking it up in a legal dictionary. Over time, this practice will help you in all aspects of your preparation.

seems to raise an issue about whether plaintiff's counsel did an adequate job of legal research to determine what he was supposed to do before filing a complaint. This may suggest to you that the issue in the case is whether plaintiff's counsel's conduct satisfied or failed to satisfy the legal category "normally competent level of legal research."

If focusing on the parties' conduct that seems to concern the court does not help, try identifying the conclusion(s) reached by the court in its opinion. A conclusion in a court opinion is often (but not always) contained in a sentence that begins with phrases such as "We **conclude** that . . . ," "We **decide** that . . . ," "We **find** that . . . ," "We **believe** that . . . ," "We **hold** that . . . ," or "We are **convinced** that . . ." Once you have identified the conclusion reached by the court, try to tie that conclusion to a legal category. In *Bridges*, for example, the opinion says: "The Court is not **convinced** that Plaintiff's counsel displayed a competent level of legal research." If you recognize this conclusion, you should be able to tie it to the legal category "normally competent level of legal research."

B. The Arguments Relied on by the Court to Resolve the First Issue in *Bridges v. Diesel*

The court concluded that plaintiff's attorney's filing of a complaint without first exhausting administrative remedies by filing a charge with the EEOC reflected a failure to engage in a "normally competent level of legal research," and therefore violated Rule 11. The court advances what might be seen as three arguments in support of its decision:

(1) A brief review of case law would have revealed the EEOC filing requirement. (This might be seen as an implicit principle argument. The court subscribes to the principle that before filing a complaint, a lawyer should generally conduct a review of the case law that is relevant to the subject matter of the complaint, and comply with the requirements of that case law. The lawyer in this case did not act in accordance with this principle.)

(2) Prior court decisions have found that failing to exhaust administrative remedies is a violation of Rule 11 for which sanctions have been awarded. (This argument may be seen as either an implicit precedent argument or an implicit argument by analogy to prior cases that have found that a failure to exhaust administrative remedies violates Rule 11 and justifies an award of sanctions under the Rule 11.)[4]

---

4. Recall that a precedent argument asserts that the same issue has previously been resolved by an authoritative source, and that the current issue should therefore be resolved in the same way. This second argument set forth in *Bridges* would be a precedent argument if the two cases referred to by the court held that a failure to file a charge with the EEOC before filing a complaint establish that a

(3) Rule 11 imposes an obligation on counsel to Stop, Think, Investigate, and Research before filing papers with the court. (This might be seen as an implicit goal argument. One of the goals of Rule 11 is to encourage lawyers to conduct adequate legal research before filing documents in federal court. In this case, the plaintiff's lawyer failed to do the sort of research that Rule 11 was intended to encourage. Therefore, a finding that plaintiff's attorney violated Rule 11 would be consistent with the purpose or goal behind Rule 11.)

1. The Benefits of Identifying the Arguments Relied on by the Court

In class, your professors will frequently ask you or a colleague questions such as: Why did the court decide the first issue as it did? What reasons did the court give for its decision? What was the court's rationale for its decision? Identifying the arguments relied on by the court in its opinion as you prepare for class will help you answer such questions and follow classroom dialogues relating to the arguments relied on by the court.

If you have identified each of the court's arguments as you prepare for class, it may then be easier for you to spot potential weaknesses or rebuttals to each argument. Identifying weaknesses and rebuttals are critical skills in law practice and, as you will see in the following chapters, you and your colleagues will sometimes be asked to practice these skills in the classroom.

To perform well on many law school exam questions and as a lawyer in practice, you must be able to make arguments to resolve issues. As you read opinions for class and identify the arguments relied on by a court to resolve an issue, you gain a sense of how to articulate legal arguments.

2. Tips for Identifying the Court's Arguments

Early in your law school career, it may be difficult to identify the arguments a court is relying on to resolve an issue. The arguments are typically not set out in a separate section of the opinion. Thus, you will seldom read an opinion with a heading in bold reading: **"Arguments and Rationales Justifying Our Decision on Issue. . . ."** In addition, the court

---

complaint was not supported by a normally competent level of legal research, and was therefore a violation of Rule 11. But the court in *Bridges* does not say that the two cases it cites involved Rule 11 or the failure to file a charge with the EEOC before filing a complaint. The prior cases may have involved a rule other than Rule 11 or may have involved a failure to exhaust administrative remedies by doing something other than failing to file a charge with the EEOC. If so, this second argument would be an argument by analogy. Recall that an argument by analogy asserts that a similar issue has previously been resolved by a respected source, and that the current issue should therefore be resolved in the same way. The two prior cases cited by the court in *Bridges* may have involved an issue similar to the one in *Bridges*. If so, the resolution of those similar issues by the court in those prior cases would be consistent with a finding in *Bridges* that the complaint was not supported by a normally competent level of legal research, and was therefore a violation of Rule 11.

does not typically employ a label to identify its arguments. Thus, the court will typically not explicitly refer to the argument types discussed in Chapter 4, not use any other label to indicate the arguments in an opinion. Nor will an opinion typically indicate where one argument ends and another begins. Instead, a court's arguments are frequently undifferentiated and intertwined with the legal rules being applied to decide the case. In some opinions it may be difficult to distinguish the court's arguments from the legal rules that it is applying.

When you have difficulty identifying a court's arguments, you can use the argument typology from Chapter 4 and ask yourself the following sorts of questions:

- Does the court say anything about the goals or purposes behind a legal rule or a legal category? Does the court say anything about whether those goals or purposes would be furthered or undermined by a resolution of an issue? Answering these questions may help to identify goal arguments.

- Does the court indicate any positive or negative consequences that might result from the resolution of an issue? Does the court indicate that it is concerned that the decision in the case will potentially affect the way people will behave in the future? Answering these questions may help to identify consequences arguments.

- Does the court make a normative statement about how things should usually happen, how documents or texts should be interpreted, how people should usually behave or how legal rules should be interpreted? Does the court make any normative criticisms of anyone's conduct? Answering these questions may help to identify principle arguments.

- Does the court refer to a similar issue that was previously resolved by other courts or authoritative sources? Does the court describe fact situations from other cases that are similar to the facts in the case before the court? Answering these questions may help to identify precedent arguments and arguments by analogy.

- Does the court refer to an inference or conclusion of fact that it is drawing? Does the court talk about the state of mind (e.g., motive, intent, etc.) of one of the parties, and the facts that determine that party's state of mind? Answering these questions may help to identify inference arguments.

C. The Second Issue in *Bridges v. Diesel* and the Arguments Relied on by the Court to Resolve the Issue

Rule 11 (c) provides that a "court may impose appropriate **sanctions** for Rule 11 (b) violations." The second issue in *Bridges* was whether the court should impose sanctions on the plaintiff's attorney for filing a complaint without first filing a charge with the EEOC.

The court decided not to sanction the plaintiff's attorney. The court relied on the following arguments to justify its decision:

(1) Rule 11 is not intended as a general fee-shifting device. (This might be seen as a goal argument. If the court had awarded sanctions, it would have been shifting the legal fees incurred by the defendant to the plaintiff. Shifting fees is <u>not</u> a goal behind Rule 11.)

(2) The prime goal of Rule 11 sanctions is deterrence of improper conduct. Plaintiff's counsel does not need to be deterred in the future because he has learned his lesson, as demonstrated by his acknowledging his error, rectifying the situation by filing a charge with the EEOC, and placing the action in suspense. (This is a prototypical goal argument. The court explains why one of the goals behind Rule 11, deterrence of improper conduct, would <u>not</u> be furthered in this case by an award of sanctions.)

(3) Rule 11 sanctions should be reserved for those exceptional circumstances in which the claim asserted is patently unmeritorious or frivolous. The mistake in the present case was procedural, rather than substantive. (This might be seen as a principle argument. The court subscribes to the principle that Rule 11 sanctions should generally be granted only when a case is obviously lacking on the merits. In this case, there has been no finding that the plaintiff's case is unmeritorious; plaintiff's counsel simply followed the incorrect procedure.)

(4) The Court is aware of the need to avoid "chilling" Title VII litigation. (This might be seen as an implicit consequences argument. If the court awards sanctions against plaintiff's counsel, other plaintiffs' counsel might be discouraged from pursuing potentially meritorious ADA claims and other meritorious claims under Title VII of federal law. The court's decision not to award sanctions avoids this negative consequence.)

D. The Legal Rules Relating to the Issues in *Bridges*

When you read an opinion for class, you are usually responsible for knowing the legal rules relating to the issues in the opinion.[5] In *Bridges*,

---

5. You may also be responsible for knowing the legal rules in assigned readings other than court opinions. If, for example, you are assigned to read portions of the text of Rule 11 in conjunction with the *Bridges* opinion, you would be responsible for knowing those provisions of Rule 11.

for example, you would probably be responsible for knowing the following legal rules from the opinion:

(1) Rule 11 is violated only if, at the time of signing, the signing of the document filed was objectively unreasonable under the circumstances.

(2) Counsel's signature certifies that a pleading is supported by a reasonable factual investigation and a normally competent level of legal research.

1. The Benefits of Identifying the Legal Rules

You derive several benefits from identifying these legal rules. First, in one type of typical law school exam question, you will be given a set of facts, but you will not be given the legal rule(s) that apply to that set of facts. Instead, you will need to know the applicable legal rule(s) to answer the exam question. The legal rule(s) that apply to a set of facts on an exam question are typically one or more of the legal rules from the opinions or other assigned materials you read for class. For example, the facts in a question on a law school examination might require you to know and apply all or a portion of the above legal rules from the *Bridges* opinion. You will not have time, however, to distill these rules from the *Bridges* opinion during the examination. You need to have identified the potentially applicable legal rules before you start the exam. In short, identifying the legal rules in court opinions as you prepare for class will help you prepare for law school exams.

The legal rules you learn as you read opinions in law school will also help you in law practice. When clients come to you with problems, they seldom bring along the applicable legal rule(s) that might solve those problems. One of your jobs as a lawyer is to identify the legal rules that might apply to the problems clients present to you. You will be better at this important skill if you leave law school with a clear understanding of a broad spectrum of the legal rules that might apply to the varied client problems you may face in law practice. Furthermore, in practice (or if you have a legal job during law school) you will frequently be required to read opinions you did not read in law school and identify the legal rules in those opinions.

Learning the legal rules as you read an opinion will also help you in the classroom. To assist you in learning the legal rules, your professors will frequently (but not always) ask you or a classmate questions about the legal rules in the opinions you have read for class. You will be better able to understand this part of the classroom dialogue if you do your best to identify the legal rules when you prepare for class.

2. Tips for Identifying the Legal Rules in a Court's Opinion

Especially early in your first year, you may have difficulty identifying the legal rules in a court's opinion. Judges frequently write opinions for an audience of experienced lawyers and other judges. They do not necessarily write opinions for the benefit of first-year law students. As a result, legal opinions are frequently not designed or intended to teach you legal rules.

In addition, a court will seldom set out in one section all the legal rules relating to the issues in the opinion; nor will a court highlight in **bold** each legal rule that it applies throughout the opinion. Instead, the legal rules are frequently dispersed and intertwined with the facts, the procedural posture of the case, and the court's reasoning. With some opinions, it can be difficult to distinguish the court's reasoning from a legal rule. (Indeed, even people with considerable experience reading opinions can sometimes reasonably disagree about what constitutes a legal rule as distinguished from the legal reasoning of the court.) For example, in *Bridges* the court's discussion of the analogy to a railroad crossing sign and the requirement to "Stop, Look and Listen" (arguably part of its reasoning) precedes its announcement of the rule that a pleading must be supported by a reasonable factual investigation and a normally competent level of legal research.

If you are having difficulty identifying the legal rules in an opinion, ask yourself one or both of the following questions:

Does the court apply or announce a "test," a set of "factors," or a "definition" that it will apply to reach a decision?

To decide an issue, does the court set out a standard that does not seem to be limited to the facts of the case before the court?

Answering these questions may help you to identify legal rules related to the issues in an opinion. In *Bridges*, for example, the court states that "Rule 11 is violated only if, at the time of signing, the signing of the document filed was objectively unreasonable under the circumstances." This appears to be a standard or test that is not limited to the facts in *Bridges*. Instead, this standard will be applied to all cases involving documents that are arguably filed in violation of Rule 11.

E. A Summary of the Facts in *Bridges*

The facts in an opinion typically consist of the pre- and post-litigation facts. Think of the pre-litigation facts as the events that occurred before the courts became involved in the case. Thus, in a typical breach of contract case, the pre-litigation facts would include what the parties did when negotiating the contract and the events that gave rise to the defendant's alleged breach of the contract. In *Bridges*, the pre-litigation facts might be summarized as follows:

> James Bridges got an attorney and his attorney determined that Mr. Bridges had a claim against Diesel Service, Inc. under the Americans with Disabilities Act. The attorney drafted a complaint against Diesel Service, Inc. Before filing the complaint, the attorney did <u>not</u> file a charge on plaintiff's behalf with the EEOC.

The post-litigation facts are the events that occurred after the court became involved in the matter. (The post-litigation facts are often referred to as the "procedural history" of the case). In *Bridges*, for instance, the post-litigation facts might be summarized as follows:

> After the attorney for plaintiff filed his complaint for violation of the ADA, the court dismissed it without prejudice for failure to exhaust administrative remedies, i.e., for failure to file a charge with the EEOC. The defendant then filed a motion asking the court to award sanctions against Plaintiff's attorney for a violation of Rule 11. The court found that Plaintiff's attorney had violated Rule 11, but declined to award sanctions.[6]

Knowing the facts in an opinion will help you in the classroom and on your law school exams.

In the classroom, a professor may ask you or your classmates about the pre-litigation and/or the post-litigation facts of a case to make sure that the pertinent facts are known by all the students in the class before discussing the court's legal analysis of the applicable legal rules. In some instances, a professor may focus on the post-litigation facts to help you understand the procedural process for resolving civil or criminal cases. In the classroom, a professor may also ask you or a colleague to critique a court opinion, to make arguments for a result directly contrary to the result in a court opinion, or to use the court opinion to make arguments by analogy. As you will see in the next few chapters, you will need to know the facts of the case to accomplish all these tasks, and to understand classroom dialogues that focus on them.

Learning the facts in an opinion as you prepare for class may also help you identify issues on an exam. For example, assume that one part of the statement of facts on a civil procedure exam mentions that a complaint was dismissed because an attorney failed to file a required notice with an administrative agency of the federal government before filing the complaint. If you know the facts of the *Bridges* case, you may

---

6. Especially early on in your first year, when you read the facts of a case you will routinely encounter words that you are unfamiliar with ("demurrer," for example). Once again, you should get in the habit of looking up such words in a legal dictionary. If you fail to do so, it may be impossible for you to understand the facts of a case.

realize that they are similar or analogous to the facts on the exam. As a result, you may realize that the facts on the exam may trigger the application of the legal rules in *Bridges*, and the facts on the exam may even involve the same legal categories. In short, knowing the facts of the cases that you read throughout a course may help you make analogical or similarity assessments to the facts on an exam. In turn, those similarity assessments may help you to identify the legal rules that potentially apply to the exam facts and the legal categories at issue on the exam.

IV. PRESERVING YOUR PREPARATION — AN ILLUSTRATIVE EXAMPLE OF A CASE BRIEF IN *BRIDGES*

This chapter has discussed why you may benefit from identifying issues, arguments, legal rules, and facts as you read a rule application opinion in preparation for class. As you identify these matters, you should preserve them in a manner that allows you ready access to them in class. You may decide to record some or all of these matters on paper or in a computer. Alternatively, you may decide to simply identify some or all of these matters with annotations, marginal notes, highlighting, or other designations directly in your textbook (this is usually referred to as "book briefing"). For example, you might indicate "first issue" in the margin of your textbook and highlight or underscore the court's arguments related to that issue.

If you wrote out your case brief in *Bridges*, it might look something like the following:

Issues and Arguments in *Bridges*

First Issue — Did plaintiff's attorney's filing of a complaint without first exhausting administrative remedies meet the requirement of "normally competent level of legal research" required by Rule 11? The court decided that it did not.

Court's Arguments Re: First Issue — (1) A brief review of case law would have revealed the EEOC filing requirement. (2) Prior court decisions have found that failing to exhaust administrative remedies is a violation of Rule 11 for which sanctions have been awarded. (3) Rule 11 imposes an obligation on counsel to Stop, Think, Investigate, and Research before filing papers with the court.

Second Issue — Should the court sanction plaintiff's attorney for violating Rule 11? The court decided not to sanction plaintiff's attorney.

Court's Arguments Re: Second Issue — (1) Rule 11 is not intended as a general fee-shifting device. (2) The prime goal of Rule 11 sanctions is deterrence of improper conduct. Plaintiff's counsel does not need to be deterred in the future because he has learned his lesson. (3) Rule 11 sanctions should be reserved for those exceptional circumstances in which the claim asserted is patently unmeritorious or frivolous. The mistake in the present case was procedural rather than substantive. (4) The court wanted to avoid chilling Title VII litigation.

Legal Rules in *Bridges*

(1) Rule 11 is violated only if, at the time of signing, the signing of the document filed was objectively unreasonable under the circumstances.

(2) Counsel's signature certifies that a pleading is supported by a reasonable factual investigation and a normally competent level of legal research.

Facts in *Bridges*

Pre-litigation facts — James Bridges got an attorney, who determined that Mr. Bridges had a claim against Diesel under the Americans with Disabilities Act. The attorney failed to file a charge on plaintiff's behalf with the EEOC.

Post-litigation facts — Plaintiff's lawyer filed a complaint against Diesel. The court dismissed it without prejudice for failure to exhaust administrative remedies. The defendant then filed a motion asking the court to award sanctions against Plaintiff's attorney for violating Rule 11. The Court denied Defendant's motion.

V. CONCLUSION

If you would like additional illustrative examples of case briefs in opinions you may be assigned in your first year, visit *www.aspenlawschool. com/books/moorebinder.*

chapter 6

Rule Application Opinions in the Classroom — Facts, Issues, Arguments, and Legal Rules

This chapter focuses on four principal topics commonly addressed in first-year classrooms when discussing and analyzing rule application opinions:

(1) the facts of the case;

(2) each issue resolved by the court;

(3) the arguments or rationale set forth in the opinion for resolving each issue; and

(4) the legal rules discussed by the court.

Not surprisingly, these topics mirror the preparation topics discussed in Chapter 5 and the entries in your case brief.

This chapter sets forth illustrative examples of classroom dialogues about each of these topics in the context of the *Bridges* opinion you read in the prior chapter. It also explains some of the reasons these topics are addressed by professors in class discussions.

Finally, the chapter explores some of the reasons professors often use a question-and-answer format in the classroom.

I. THE FACTS OF A CASE

Through a combination of lecture and/or questions, a professor will routinely focus the class's attention on the facts in the court's opinion.[1]

1. Q: Mr. Munzer, after James Bridges and his attorney talked about why he was discharged, what did the plaintiff's lawyer do next?

2. A: He filed a complaint in federal court.

---

1. The hypothetical professor depicted in this chapter and Chapters 7–9 uses primarily a question-and-answer approach. By illustrating this approach exclusively, we do not mean to suggest that the question-and-answer approach is necessarily the best teaching method. It is, however, a common approach to first-year classroom discussions.

3. Q: Let's go back a bit. Before he filed the complaint, did he do anything other than talk to his client and prepare the complaint?

4. A: I'm not sure.

5. Q: Do we know from the opinion whether he did any legal research about the requirement for age discrimination complaints?

6. A: I don't think he did, because the court says that if he had done any research he should have found out about the requirement that he file a charge with the EEOC?

7. Q: Where does it say in the opinion that the plaintiff's lawyer failed to do legal research regarding the need to file a charge with the EEOC before filing the complaint?

8. A: It doesn't say that exactly.

9. Q: Do we know from the opinion whether plaintiff's lawyer didn't know about the requirement that he file a charge before filing the complaint or he knew about the requirement that he file a charge but just neglected to file one?

10. A: I can't tell from the opinion.

11. Q: All right, after he filed the complaint, what happened?

12. A: The court dismissed his complaint for failure to file a charge with the EEOC.

13. Q: Before the court dismissed the complaint, did the defendant do anything to bring to the court's attention that plaintiff's lawyer had failed to file a charge with the EEOC?

14. A: I don't know.

15. Q: Well, let's talk about what might have happened between the time the plaintiff filed the complaint and the time the court dismissed it. . . .

In this example, the dialogue begins by focusing on the pre-litigation facts in *Bridges* (Nos. 1–10). A professor may begin the class discussion of an opinion with such questions for several reasons. First, a professor may want the entire class to have a general understanding of the facts before moving on to the issues resolved in the opinion. Second, a professor may want to make you sensitive to the fact that court opinions sometimes omit potentially relevant facts (Nos. 3–10).

After several questions about the pre-litigation facts, the dialogue then shifts to explore the post-litigation facts (Nos. 11–15). A professor may discuss the post-litigation facts to help you learn the procedural process applicable to civil or criminal litigation. For example, a professor might use the *Bridges* opinion to explore the procedural steps that are typically followed to bring Rule 11 violations to the attention of a court.

II. THE ISSUE(S) AND THE ARGUMENTS RELIED ON BY THE COURT TO RESOLVE THEM

Classroom dialogues routinely focus on the issue(s) addressed by the court in its opinion, and the arguments the court relies on to resolve them.

1. Q: Mr. Yeazell, let's put aside the question of sanctions for the moment. On the question of the violation of Rule 11 what was the issue before the court in *Bridges*?

2. A: Whether plaintiff's counsel violated Rule 11 by filing a complaint without first filing a charge with the EEOC?

3. Q: And how did the court resolve that issue?

4. A: The court says that it was a violation.

5. Q: And what requirement of Rule 11 did the court say plaintiff's lawyer violated by filing a complaint without first filing a charge with the EEOC?

6. A: The court says that if a complaint is not supported by a normally competent level of legal research, it violates Rule 11. And, Plaintiff didn't do a competent level of legal research before he filed the complaint.

7. Q: Does the court explain why a lawyer doing a competent job of legal research would have found out about the requirement of first filing a charge with EEOC?

8. A: Well, the court says that a brief review of the case law would tell a lawyer that a charge had to be filed. So I guess the court is saying it is not a competent job of legal research if a lawyer doesn't at least spend a little time reviewing the relevant cases before filing a complaint.

9. Q: Does the court provide any other explanations for why it concludes that plaintiff's lawyer didn't do a competent job of legal research?

10. A: I don't think so.

11. Q: Well, right after saying that a brief review of case law would have revealed the need to file a charge with the EEOC, the court

says, "Further, an award of sanctions for failure to exhaust administrative remedies is not unprecedented." What does that language indicate, Ms. Freemont?

12. A: I guess it means that other lawyers have been sanctioned for not exhausting administrative remedies.

13. Q: And why do you think the court said that in the opinion? After all, it did not sanction the lawyer in this case.

14. A: Well, I think the court is saying that plaintiff's lawyer in this case didn't exhaust administrative remedies, and in prior cases other lawyers have violated Rule 11 and have been sanctioned for the same sort of conduct. So, I think the court is saying that prior courts have found the failure to exhaust administrative remedies violated Rule 11. I suppose that's another explanation or rational for the court's decision plaintiff's lawyer violated Rule 11 in this case.

In this exchange, Nos. 1–6 bring out the first issue in *Bridges*. Nos. 7–14 bring out some of the arguments relied on by the *Bridges* court to resolve the first issue relating to the violation of Rule 11. Professors will not necessarily use the term "arguments" in classroom dialogues, however. Instead, as discussed in Chapter 4 and illustrated in the above example, a professor may ask for the "rationale," the "justification," or the "explanation" for the court's resolution of the issue.

As discussed in the prior chapter, if you read court opinions in law practice you will be required to identify issues and the arguments relied on by the court to resolve them. Professors routinely provide the class with opportunities to practice these crucial skills when analyzing opinions in the classroom.

III. MAKING A COURT'S ARGUMENT MORE EXPLICIT

The arguments in court opinions are frequently stated implicitly. Courts use implicitly stated arguments for at least two reasons. First, being implicit may be more efficient. Explicit arguments take more time and effort, and the experienced lawyers in a case can frequently understand implicit arguments as well as they can explicit ones. An implicit argument can also be efficient when the court thinks that the resolution of an issue is relatively obvious, and therefore the opinion should spend as little time as possible on that issue. Second, judges are busy and they may not take as much time as they should to clearly and expressly articulate their arguments.

In class dialogues, a professor may require you or a colleague to make a court's implicitly stated argument more explicit. The dialogue below illustrates how a professor might require students to make more explicit one of the Bridges' court's arguments on the sanctions issue.

1. Q: The court finds that the plaintiff's lawyer violated Rule 11. Mr. Prager, why doesn't the court sanction him for his violation?

2. A: Because the plaintiff's lawyer acknowledged his mistake and filed a charge with the EEOC.

3. Q: Well, the violation of Rule 11 occurred when plaintiff's lawyer filed the complaint, so why does what he did later have anything to do with whether he should be sanctioned?

4. A: Well, his actions were designed to rectify his error.

5. Q: Why should that matter? The violation of Rule 11 occurred when he filed the complaint, so why does what he did later have anything to do with whether he should be sanctioned?

6. A: I'm not sure.

7. Q: Well, maybe we can make the court's argument more explicit. Does the court say anything about the purpose of sanctions?

8. A: I think the court says sanctions in this case are not necessary to deter future misconduct, so I guess one purpose of sanctions is to deter future misconduct.

9. Q: Mr. Prager has identified for us one of the purposes behind Rule 11 that the court seems to be relying on, at least in part, to support its decision. So, Mr. Prager, why does the court conclude that sanctions are not necessary to deter future misconduct by plaintiff's counsel?

10. A: The courts says that it thinks plaintiff's counsel has learned his lesson and will demonstrate greater diligence in the future, so the court does not need to award sanctions to achieve the purpose of deterring future misconduct by plaintiff's lawyer.

11. Q: Mr. Bergman, is that the court's only justification for the decision not to award sanctions?

12. A: The court also says that Rule 11 is not a fee-shifting device.

13. Q: Well, let's talk about that. . . .

In this example, the initial student responses (Nos. 1–6) do not provide an explicit statement of the court's argument that sanctions are not necessary to achieve the goal of deterring future violations of Rule 11 by plaintiff's counsel. That is, these initial responses do not explicitly set out the goal mentioned by the court, nor do these initial responses explicitly state the court's explanation of why sanctions are not necessary to further that goal. The professor then helps the students make the court's argument more explicit (Nos. 7–10).

Stating arguments explicitly is an essential skill that you need to learn. In law practice, if you are not explicit, judges and adversaries may fail to fully understand or appreciate the persuasive power of your argument. Professors will provide you with opportunities to learn this essential skill by routinely requiring you to explicitly articulate the implicit arguments made in court opinions. As you become more familiar with legal arguments and have multiple opportunities to practice (and watch your colleagues practice in class), you will become more skilled at turning a court's implicit arguments into explicit ones, and making explicit arguments when asked to do so by a professor.

The remainder of the dialogue (Nos. 11–13) begins to surface a second goal argument discussed by the court in support of its decision. Of course, during class discussions a professor may not address every argument in a court opinion.

IV. THE LEGAL RULES IN THE COURT'S OPINION

A professor will also use classroom dialogues to bring out the legal rules mentioned in the court's opinion and any supplemental readings assigned for the class. The professor may do so even if the legal rules do not raise an issue in the opinion.

1. Q: Mr. Messinger, let's talk about where the "normally competent level of legal research" language in *Bridges* came from. Looking just at the text of Rule 11, what sort of investigation does a lawyer have to make before filing a complaint to comply with Rule 11?

2. A: Rule 11 says the lawyer has to make a reasonable inquiry under the circumstances before filing the complaint to determine if the complaint is warranted by existing law and if the allegations in the complaint are supported by evidence.

3. Q: Does the *Bridges* opinion elaborate on the meaning of this "reasonable inquiry under the circumstances" language in Rule 11?

4. A: The court says that the inquiry must be objectively reasonable. A lawyer can't use the pure heart and an empty head defense.

5. Q: And where did this "objective" language come from?

6. A: The court seems to use the *Ford Motor Co. v. Summit Motor Products* case as the authority for the fact that the inquiry must be objectively reasonable. So, I suppose that language came from that case.

7. Q: And does the *Bridges* court say anything about what constitutes an objectively reasonable inquiry?

8. A: I think the court says it is objectively reasonable if the complaint is supported by a reasonable factual investigation and a normally competent level of legal research.

9. Q: Where did the "supported by a reasonable factual investigation and a normally competent level of legal research" language come from?

10. A: I think that language came from the case of *Lieb v. Topstone Industries*. Because the opinion seems to use *Lieb* as authority for that language.

11. Q: So the "reasonable inquiry under the circumstances" language in Rule 11 has been defined by a court opinion to mean an "objectively reasonable inquiry," and an objectively reasonable inquiry has been defined to mean that a complaint is supported by "a reasonable factual investigation and a normally competent level of legal research." Let's talk about why prior court opinions have defined some of the requirements or categories in Rule 11. Ms. Scott, why do you think prior court opinions defined the "reasonable inquiry under the circumstances" language in Rule 11?

This dialogue brings out some of the legal rules discussed in the *Bridges* opinion and in the text of Rule 11. Portions of the dialogue also illustrate that some of the rules stated in the *Bridges* opinion were first announced by or based upon previously decided cases (Nos. 5 and 6 and 9 and 10). This part of the dialogue may help the class understand the evolution of the legal rules in this area.

V. WHY PROFESSORS ASK QUESTIONS

At some point in your first year, you might reasonably say to yourself something like the following:

"Why does the professor ask so many questions? Why doesn't the professor simply tell me things like the important facts of the case, the issues in the case, the arguments supporting the court's decision, and the legal rules announced in the opinion? Why tease out these matters by asking novice first-year law students questions they often struggle to answer?

The client problems you encounter in law practice will routinely involve different legal rules and factual scenarios than those in the court opinions you read in law school. Consequently, in practice you will have to do more than recall the legal rules and legal arguments you learned in law school. In law practice, you will have to analyze court opinions on your own to advise clients on alternative courses of action, to respond to inquiries from senior lawyers working with you on cases, and to make arguments during settlement negotiations and in court hearings.[2] Analyzing court opinions is a complex skill. To learn to do it, you need to practice doing it repeatedly, in many cases and in different legal areas. You will also need repeated feedback on your performance.[3] The feedback you receive in the classroom is usually in the form of a follow-up question from the professor. Such follow-up questions frequently require you to refine your analysis or give you immediate opportunities to improve your performance.[4] Thus, the question-and-answer format commonly used in a first-year classroom is designed, in part, to put you in the role of a lawyer and provide you with repeated practice and feedback on your analysis of court opinions.[5]

In addition, you will frequently be given a set of facts on a law school exam. You will then routinely be required to identify the legal rules that apply to those facts, to break the legal rules into categories, and spot issues. Furthermore, many examinations will require you to construct your own arguments to resolve issues. The question-and-answer format in the classroom provides you with practice and feedback on the skills involved in breaking legal rules into legal categories, spotting issues, and constructing arguments.

In sum, if a professor simply lectured you on the results of the professor's own analysis of a court opinion, you and your classmates would have little opportunity to practice many of the basic skills you will need in law practice and on law school examinations. Thus, you should embrace the learning opportunities presented by well-formed and well-organized classroom questions requiring you to analyze court opinions.

---

2. In addition, some states' bar examinations may give you court opinions and ask you to apply them to a client's problem.

3. It is usually difficult to acquire competency in any complex skill without significant opportunities for practice and feedback on your efforts. Imagine, for example, trying to learn to play the piano or write expositive prose simply by reading or listening to a series of lectures on "how to do it."

4. This feedback aspect of follow-up questions may be difficult to recognize because, unlike most feedback, it occurs in a very public setting and is sometimes delivered in a critical tone.

5. An individual professor may have many other motives for relying on a question-and-answer format in the classroom. For example, some professors may think this format of the classroom helps to make you a proactive learner and will improve your analytical skills in all areas.

VI. WHY PROFESSORS DON'T ANSWER QUESTIONS

A professor will sometimes respond to a question from you or a classmate with a direct and definitive answer. Many times, however, a professor will decline to directly answer a question and instead respond by saying something like: "Well, what do you think?" A professor may provide a "what do you think" response for many reasons. Frequently, however, a professor provides such a response to give you practice in thinking through answers on your own. In short, professors sometimes decline to answer questions for the same reason they pose them initially: to give you practice doing what you will be required to do on your own in law practice and on examinations.

chapter 7

Rule Application Opinions in the Classroom — Critiquing a Court's Arguments

Professors will sometimes orchestrate the class discussion to critique the arguments relied on by a court to resolve an issue. This chapter sets out two examples of classroom dialogues directed at such a critique in *Bridges*, and explains some of the reasons professors will frequently ask you or your classmates to critique a court's arguments.

I. EXAMPLE #1

As you will recall, one of the arguments relied on by the court in *Bridges* to justify its decision not to award sanctions against plaintiff's attorney was the following:

> Rule 11 sanctions should be reserved for those exceptional circumstances where the claim asserted is patently unmeritorious or frivolous. The mistake in the present case was procedural rather than substantive. . . .

The dialogue below illustrates one way in which a professor might critique this argument.

1. Q: Ms. Koehler, you have correctly pointed out that one of the reasons the court says it decided not to award sanctions against plaintiff's attorney was because sanctions should be reserved for claims that are patently unmeritorious or frivolous. And, the court says that plaintiff's attorney's mistake was procedural because he failed to file a charge before filing a complaint. What do you think of this argument Ms. Koehler?

2. A: I'm not sure. It seems to make sense to me. It's not like he filed a bogus case, he just got things in the wrong order and that shouldn't justify sanctioning him.

3. Q: What is the purpose or goal that sanctions are designed to further?

4. A: The court says that sanctions are designed to deter future misconduct.

5. Q: Well, if that's the purpose of sanctions, why should it matter if the violation of Rule 11 was procedural? Don't we want to deter future misconduct relating to procedural errors?

6. A: I suppose we do want to do that, but in this case he acknowledged and corrected his error.

7. Q: Doesn't the text of Rule 11 suggest that sanctions are designed, at least in part, to deter future conduct of others who are similarly situated?

8. A: It does say that.

9. Q: Well, Ms. Koehler, assume we are three years down the road and you are a lawyer practicing in the federal court. You read an opinion sanctioning a lawyer under Rule 11 for failing to follow proper procedures. Do you think that would encourage you to follow proper procedures in federal court?

10. A: I suppose it would. But even without those sanctions, I'd try to follow proper procedures.

11. Q: And even without sanctions you'd try not to file unmeritorious claims, correct?

12. A: Yes.

13. Q: So lawyers generally try to both follow proper procedures and avoid unmeritorious claims even without sanctions. So when we consider sanctions, why should it matter if the mistake is procedural or substantive?

14. A: It just seems like a more serious error to file an unmeritorious claim than to get things in the wrong order.

15. Q: Well, let's talk about that. Don't both kinds of errors end up wasting the court's time and the time of an opposing party and their lawyer?

16. A: I guess that's true, but . . .

The professor begins this dialogue by asking a student to opine about one of the arguments relied on by the court. The professor then points out that one of the goals of the sanctions provisions in Rule 11 (deterring future misconduct) might be furthered if lawyers were sanctioned for procedural as well as substantive errors (Nos. 3–6). Professors will sometimes ask you about the goals behind the rules being applied by a court and then orchestrate a dialogue to explore whether the court's decision is consistent or inconsistent with these goals. These dialogues help you to identify goals and provide you with practice making and critiquing goal arguments.

The professor brings out an additional goal behind Rule 11, namely, deterring future misconduct of similarly situated lawyers (Nos. 7–8). The professor then poses a hypothetical factual scenario to the student to illustrate that the goal of deterring future misconduct of similarly situated lawyers might be furthered by sanctioning the plaintiff's lawyer in *Bridges* (Nos. 9–10). Thus, the exchange develops a goal argument in favor of sanctions and calls into question the court's argument that mere procedural errors should not be sanctioned under Rule 11. Professors will often use hypothetical factual scenarios (called "hypos" or "hypotheticals") to facilitate the critique of a court's argument.

Next, the professor orchestrates the dialogue to question whether the imposition of sanctions ought to turn on the distinction between substantive or procedural errors, because conscientious lawyers will try to adhere to both requirements even in the absence of any sanctions (Nos. 10–14).

Finally, the professor begins to address the question of whether substantive and procedural errors have similar negative consequences (Nos. 15–16). If they have similar negative consequences, it may again call into question the court's suggestion that substantive errors should justify sanctions but procedural errors should not.

II. EXAMPLE #2

A second argument relied on by the court in *Bridges* to justify its decision not to award sanctions against plaintiff's attorney was the following:

> . . . the Court is aware of the need to avoid "chilling" Title VII litigation. . . .

The dialogue below illustrates one way in which a professor might structure a classroom dialogue to critique this argument.

1. Q: Mr. Rader, the court argues that it does not want to award sanctions against plaintiff's attorney because sanctions might "chill" Title VII litigation. Do you agree with that argument?

2. A: I hadn't really thought about it. I assumed the court knew what it was talking about.

3. Q: Well, let's think about it now. What do you think "chill" means?

4. A: I think it means discourage. So I think the court is saying that if sanctions were awarded they might discourage other lawyers from filing similar suits.

5. Q: I also think that's what the court is saying. Do you think the court's reasoning here is persuasive?

6. A: I have no idea.

7. Q: Does anyone else have any thoughts about this? Yes, Ms. Schmalholtz.

8. A: I don't think the argument makes any sense. If a lawyer thinks she has a good case she is going to file it; she's not going to sit in her office with what she thinks is a perfectly good case and say, "I better not file this, I might get sanctioned." She'll just try her best to research the requirements, comply with them, and then file the case. That's what she'll do whether or not sanctions are awarded in *Bridges*.

9. Q: Suppose the court in *Bridges* did sanction the plaintiff's lawyer. Now assume that a lawyer who is not familiar with the requirements of Title VII litigation has a client come into her office with a questionable Title VII claim. Might she say to herself, "This is a close case and I really don't know this area of the law. And, I read that *Bridges* case and you can get sanctioned for not following all the requirements in Title VII cases. I don't think I want to file this case." What do you think, Ms. Schmalholtz?

10. A: I suppose it's possible. But *Bridges* involved a procedural matter, and the lawyer you describe is concerned about the merits of her case. So I think it is more likely that . . .

In this example, the dialogue first makes explicit the court's consequences argument that an award of sanctions would "chill" Title VII litigation (Nos. 1–4). The professor then asks the class to opine about the persuasiveness of this argument (Nos. 5–7). In essence, the professor asks the class whether the negative consequence of discouraging meritorious lawsuits is likely to occur. Ms. Schmalholtz's answer provides a hypothetical that suggests that awarding sanctions in *Bridges* may <u>not</u> result in the chilling of other Title VII litigation (No. 8). Having elicited this student critique of the courts "chilling" argument, the professor's next question poses another hypothetical that suggests that the student's critique may be subject to a counterargument (No. 9). In essence, the professor has tried to support the court's argument by suggesting in some instances an award of sanctions in *Bridges* might indeed deter the filing of meritorious claims in the future. Ms. Schmalholtz's final answer in the dialogue concedes that the professor's suggested counter-argument may have some validity, but also starts to provide a counter to the counter.

III. WHY PROFESSORS CRITIQUE THE ARGUMENTS IN COURT OPINIONS

You might reasonably ask why a professor takes class time to engage you in a critique of the arguments in court opinions. At this early stage of your legal career, you may have your hands full just trying to identify the legal rules, issues, and arguments discussed in a court's opinion. Asking you to critique the reasoning of the experienced jurist(s) who wrote the opinion may seem beyond your ken at this point in your career. Moreover, the critique will not change anything in the court's opinion. Nevertheless, while it may be difficult for you to learn to critique the arguments in court opinions, a professor may have several legitimate reasons for asking you to do so.

One critically important skill you need as a practicing lawyer is the ability to point out weaknesses or flaws in arguments made by an adversary. The arguments made by your adversaries in practice will be the same types of arguments made by courts in their opinions. For example, your opponent may rely on a principle or consequences argument during a negotiation session, a settlement conference, or in court. Classroom critiques of the arguments in court opinions are designed, in part, to help you learn to spot flaws or shortcomings in an adversary's argument. When you learn to recognize these flaws and shortcomings, you can point them out to a court. Similarly, when an adversary relies on an opinion in which a court's arguments are flawed, you can suggest that a court disregard an adversary's argument because it relies on a flawed opinion. Finally, as you learn to recognize argument flaws you should be better able to eliminate or minimize them in your own arguments.

As discussed in Chapter 6, to learn the complex skill of critiquing legal arguments, you need repeated practice doing it and repeated feedback on your performance. The question-and-answer format frequently used in the law school classroom is designed, in part, to put you in the role of a lawyer and provide you with the necessary practice and feedback on this critical skill.

Classroom critiques of court opinions may also help you learn to overcome cognitive dissonance. People have a tendency to strongly commit to the first arguments they hear on an issue, especially when those arguments resonate with strongly held values or beliefs. This initial commitment may be especially likely to occur when you are a beginning law student and you assume that the judge who wrote the opinion "knows the law." Consequently, when you first read a court's opinion, you may become strongly committed to the arguments articulated by a court in favor of its decision. Cognitive dissonance may then make it difficult for you to identify and fairly evaluate critiques of the court's arguments. Repeated classroom critiques in your first-year classes may help you to learn to overcome or mitigate the effects of cognitive dissonance.

Classroom critiques may also help you to recognize that you can, at the same time, both accept and criticize the result and the reasoning in a court opinion. In *Bridges*, for example, absent an appeal to a higher court, the legal system accepts the result reached by the court as final. And, if the *Bridges* case is not overruled by a higher court, you can use the result in *Bridges*, as well as the court's arguments justifying its decision, when arguing about how future cases should be decided. At the same time, you can explore the question of whether the court in *Bridges* perhaps should have reached a different result. In other words, although our legal system gives certain effects to judicial opinions, you need not subscribe to the notion that opinions, or the judges who write them, are necessarily normatively correct.

Finally, repeatedly critiquing a court's arguments in class can help you develop what might be called a skeptical habit of mind. When you develop a skeptical habit of mind you recognize that **all legal arguments, whether made by you, an adversary, a court, or a professor, are routinely subject to counterarguments and critiques**. If you develop a skeptical habit of mind, when evaluating an argument that you or someone else makes or might make, you should feel comfortable employing the argument typology in Chapter 4 and asking yourself questions such as the following:

- Is that really a goal behind the rule? Will that goal be furthered and, if so, by how much, by a decision for one of the parties in this case?

- How do we know that that consequence will really happen and, if so, to what extent? Is that consequence positive or negative?

- Is that really a generally accepted principle and will it be furthered by a decision for one of the parties in this case?

- Is an analogy apt, or are there ways to distinguish it? Are there other analogies that point in the opposite direction?

- Does the circumstantial evidence justify the proposed inference? Is there another inference that might be drawn from the evidence?

For all the reasons discussed above, a professor may structure a classroom dialogue to critique the arguments in an opinion whether or not she thinks the reasoning of the court is persuasive and whether or not she believes the court reached the correct result.

chapter 8

Rule Application Opinions in the Classroom — What Constitutes a Holding

I. WHAT IS A "HOLDING" IN A RULE APPLICATION OPINION?

A professor will sometimes ask you about a court's "holding" or "holdings" in a rule application opinion. There is no one precise, generally accepted definition of the term "holding." In cases involving rule application, our definition of a holding of a case is: a statement of a court's decision regarding the issue in the case. Under this definition, the holding in *Bridges* with respect to the violation of Rule 11 might be stated as follows:

Holding Re: Violation of Rule 11 — Version #1 Rule 11's requirement that a lawyer engage in a normally competent level of legal research is violated when a lawyer files an ADA complaint without first filing a charge with the EEOC.

This holding incorporates the facts (the lawyer files an ADA complaint without first filing a charge with the EEOC) and the legal category ("normally competent level of legal research") creating the first issue in *Bridges*, and the court's decision on how the issue should be resolved.

This is not the only way one might state a holding in *Bridges* with respect to the violation of Rule 11. Another version of the holding might be stated as follows:

Holding Re: Violation of Rule 11 — Version #2 Rule 11's requirement that a lawyer engage in a normally competent level of legal research is violated when a lawyer files a complaint without first exhausting administrative remedies.

This version of the holding incorporates the same legal category (a "normally competent level of legal research") as version #1. However, in version #2 the facts are characterized as "when a lawyer files a complaint without first exhausting administrative remedies." This holding contains a different and slightly broader characterization of the facts than version #1 ("when a lawyer files an ADA complaint without first filing a charge with the EEOC"). The broader characterization makes version #2 of the holding broader than version #1. Version #1 is limited to ADA complaints and a failure to file a charge with the EEOC. Version #2 potentially encompasses any type of complaint and any conduct that fails to exhaust administrative remedies.

A third version of the holding in *Bridges* with respect to the violation of Rule 11 might be stated as follows:

Holding Re: Violation of Rule 11 — Version #3 Rule 11's requirement that a lawyer engage in a normally competent level of legal research is violated when a lawyer files a complaint without first complying with any pre-filing requirements.

Version #3 of the holding is slightly broader than version #2. Version #2 is limited to administrative remedies, and version #3 encompasses any conduct that fails to exhaust administrative remedies <u>as well as</u> any conduct that fails to fulfill any other pre-filing requirements.

A fourth version of the holding in *Bridges* with respect to the violation of Rule 11 might be stated as follows:

Holding Re: Violation of Rule 11 — Version #4 Rule 11's requirement that a lawyer engage in a normally competent level of legal research is violated whenever a lawyer files any document with a court without first complying with any pre-filing requirements.

Version #4 of the holding is significantly broader than version #3. Version #3 is limited to complaints filed with a court, while version #4 encompasses the filing of any document (e.g., answers to complaints, motions of any type, affidavits, legal briefs, etc.).

Judges, lawyers, and law professors can reasonably disagree about what is a legitimate way to state the holding in a case. We believe that most members of the legal profession agree that a holding in a rule application case should generally be limited or confined to the specific facts creating the issue resolved by the court.[1] Applying that standard, version #1 above might be the only legitimate statement of the holding in *Bridges*. Other members of the legal profession might accept either version #1 or #2 as legitimate, but few would accept version #3 or #4 as a legitimate statement of the holding in *Bridges*.

Because a court opinion can resolve more than one issue, an opinion can have multiple holdings. In *Bridges*, for example, the court also resolves the question of whether the facts fall inside or outside the "sanctions appropriate" legal category. This holding might be stated as follows:

---

1. As you will see in Part Two, the holdings in cases creating new legal rules go well beyond the facts creating an issue.

Holding Re: Monetary Sanctions Under Rule 11 — Version #1
When plaintiff's counsel violates Rule 11 by failing to file a charge with the EEOC before filing an ADA complaint, monetary sanctions are not appropriate when plaintiff's counsel immediately acknowledges his error, attempts to rectify the situation by filing a charge with the EEOC, and moves to place the action in civil suspense.

Version #1 is a narrow holding because it is limited to the specific facts in *Bridges.* A broader statement of the holding on the issue of sanctions might be as follows:

Holding Re: Monetary Sanctions Under Rule 11 — Version #2
When plaintiff's counsel violates Rule 11 by failing to comply with pre-filing requirements, monetary sanctions are not appropriate when plaintiff's counsel takes timely steps to correct pre-filing errors.

Version #2 is broader than version #1 because it characterizes the facts more generally. Again, the narrower holding in version #1 is more likely to be accepted as a legitimate holding than the broader holding in version #2.

II. THE LEGAL EFFECT OF A HOLDING

The holding of a case is important, in part, because it can serve as binding precedent. For example, assume for the moment that the *Bridges* opinion was written by the U. S. Supreme Court. The holding in *Bridges* would then be binding precedent in all federal courts in the United States.[2] That is, all federal courts would be required to follow the holdings in *Bridges* when deciding future cases.

III. CLASSROOM DISCUSSION OF A HOLDING

The dialogue below illustrates one way in which a professor might explore one of the holdings in *Bridges* and its precedential effect.

1. Q: Mr. Robinson, what is the holding of the court in *Bridges* regarding the violation of Rule 11?

2. A: The court held that when you file an ADA complaint without first filing a charge with the EEOC, you violate Rule 11.

---

2. We do not address here the rules controlling the question of which courts are bound by the holding of a particular case. This question will, however, be addressed in at least one of your first-year courses.

3. Q: What requirements or categories in Rule 11 would be violated?

4. A: The requirement that you engage in a competent level of legal research before you file the complaint.

5. Q: Well, Mr. Robinson, let's test that holding just a bit. I want you to assume for the moment that *Bridges* was decided by the U. S. Supreme Court. I also want you to assume that you are the defendant's lawyer in the following case: Plaintiff filed a complaint against your client alleging discrimination in employment based on race under Title VII. The plaintiff's lawyer was required to file a charge with the EEOC before filing the complaint, but neglected to do so. As defendant's lawyer, you have filed a motion pursuant to Rule 11 seeking sanctions against plaintiff's attorney. Can you say to the court that the *Bridges* decision constitutes binding precedent that requires the court to find that the plaintiff's lawyer in your case violated Rule 11?

6. A: Yes.

7. Q: But you told us just a moment ago that the holding in *Bridges* applied to ADA complaints and the case I have posed to you involved a race discrimination complaint. So how can you say the holding in *Bridges* constitutes binding precedent?

8. A: I don't think the type of complaint involved was important to the decision in *Bridges.* I think what was critical was that the charge had to be filed with the EEOC before the complaint was filed. Those were the critical facts in *Bridges* and those facts are present in my case, so I think the holding in *Bridges* controls.

9. Q: Let's assume that you are correct and the holding in *Bridges* is controlling. Now let's change the facts of our hypothetical just a bit, then. Assume in your case that before filing the complaint the plaintiff's lawyer was required to file a notice of intent to file a complaint rather than a charge, and that that notice had to be filed with a new government agency called the "Treat Employees Fairly Commission," usually referred to as the TEFC. Would the holding in *Bridges* still be binding precedent in your case?

10. A: I'm not sure. I suppose it would depend on how broadly the holding in *Bridges* was interpreted. If I could convince the judge in my case that the holding in *Bridges* was that a failure to file a required document with a government agency before filing a complaint constituted a violation of Rule 11, it would still be binding precedent.

11. Q: How would you go about trying to convince a judge to accept this broader holding in *Bridges*?

12. A: I'd argue that the broad holding was a legitimate interpretation of the court's opinion.

13. Q: What arguments would you make in support of your position?

14. A: Well, first I'd argue that . . .[3]

In this example, the professor elicits one statement of a holding in *Bridges* (Nos. 1–4). In No. 5, the professor gives the student a hypothetical to explore whether the student's statement of the holding in *Bridges* would be binding precedent in the hypothetical. Hypotheticals are one of professors' favorite vehicles for asking students to think about the scope of binding precedent. In No. 7, the professor asks the student to justify his position that *Bridges* would be binding precedent in the hypothetical, and in No. 8 the student justifies his answer. In No. 9, the professor provides a new hypothetical requiring the student to argue for a broader holding in *Bridges.* The final portions of the dialogue then begin to address the arguments that might be made for such a holding.

---

3. We have not addressed the question of how you might construct arguments to convince a court that it should accept your characterization of the holding in a case. You will undoubtedly address this sort of question in some of your first-year courses. Such arguments would, however, typically be of the same type as the arguments discussed in Chapter 4.

chapter 9

Rule Application Opinions in the Classroom — Making Arguments to Resolve New Issues

A professor will frequently give the class a hypothetical new case that creates an opportunity for students to make arguments relating to new issues created by the hypothetical. The new issues will frequently relate to one or more of the legal categories in the rules applied by the court in the opinion assigned for class. For example, after discussing the *Bridges* opinion in class, a professor might provide a hypothetical case creating one or more new issues in the legal rules applied by the court in *Bridges*. After setting out the facts of the hypothetical, a professor will ask a student to assume the role of a lawyer for one of the parties in the hypothetical case. The professor will then ask that student to make arguments for her client on the new issue. Below you will find three examples of such interchanges.

This chapter concludes with a brief explanation of how classroom dialogues relating to hypotheticals also provide you with practice for law school exams.

I. EXAMPLE #1 — "DRAGGING AND DROPPING" — USING THE ARGUMENTS IN A COURT OPINION TO MAKE ARGUMENTS IN A NEW CASE

One skill you need to learn in your first year is how to apply or transfer the arguments from a court opinion to an issue in a new case. You will frequently draw on this skill when making argument for clients in law practice. For example, in law practice assume you represent a client charged with violating Rule 11. You might use one or more arguments in the *Bridges* opinion to try to convince a judge that opposing counsel violated Rule 11.

"Drag and drop" is one technique for applying the arguments from a court opinion to a new case. This technique is similar to the approach for moving information in a computer from one file to another. When you use this technique, you drag arguments from a court opinion and drop them on the facts of the new case. You then explain why the arguments from the court opinion make sense when resolving an issue in the new case. The following example illustrates how a professor might require you to use this drag-and-drop approach and provide you with feedback on your efforts.

1. Q: [Professor] Let's assume the following set of facts: Ms. Fibber came into the office of Mr. Quicklawyer late one afternoon and said that she was injured in an auto accident two days earlier when her car was struck by a truck owned by Outofstate Trucking Co. After interviewing Ms. Fibber, the next morning Mr. Quicklawyer filed a complaint in federal court against Outofstate alleging that the negligence of the driver of the Outofstate truck caused the accident and the resulting personal injuries to Ms. Fibber. The lawyer for Outofstate filed an answer denying any liability.

   Three days after the answer was filed, Mr. Quicklawyer discovered that his client had not told him the truth about the accident, and that Outofstate had not been involved in the accident at all. The Outofstate driver had simply stopped at the scene of the accident to see if he could help Ms. Fibber. Mr. Quicklawyer then immediately filed a motion to dismiss his complaint. The judge in the case then set a hearing to determine if Quicklawyer's filing of the complaint violated Rule 11 and if Quicklawyer should be sanctioned for any such violation.

   At the hearing, the court held that Quicklawyer had violated Rule 11 because he failed to make a reasonable factual investigation to determine if the allegations in his complaint had evidentiary support. The judge delayed until tomorrow the argument on the question of whether Quicklawyer should be sanctioned for his violation of Rule 11.

   Ms. Damion, assume that you are an associate in Quicklawyer's office and you are assigned to appear in court and argue against the award of sanctions. I want you to assume that the *Bridges* opinion was written by the U.S. Supreme Court; can you make any use of the *Bridges* opinion to argue that Quicklawyer should not be sanctioned?

2. A: Well, I'm not sure how I could use *Bridges* to argue for Quicklawyer. The facts of *Bridges* are different from those in Quicklawyer, and *Bridges* involved a different issue. *Bridges* involved the failure to do competent legal research, and the Quicklawyer case seems to involve a failure to conduct a reasonable factual investigation. So I don't think the holding in *Bridges* controls in Quicklawyer.

3. Q: Well, let's assume that you are correct and that the holding in *Bridges* does not control here. Perhaps we can look at the rationale

for the decision in *Bridges* and see if it makes sense in Quicklawyer. Ms. Damion, can you remember the court's rationale for its decision in *Bridges*?

4. A: Well, the court in *Bridges* based its decision not to award sanctions at least in part on the fact that the plaintiff's lawyer in that case immediately acknowledged his error, so sanctions were not necessary to further the goal of deterring future misconduct.

5. Q: All right. Let's take that argument and see if it makes sense in the Quicklawyer case. What do you think, Ms. Damion?

6. A: Well, Quicklawyer sought to dismiss the complaint as soon as he learned it was not meritorious. Furthermore, just like the lawyer in *Bridges*, Quicklawyer has probably learned his lesson because he has had to waste his time drafting and filing a complaint and a motion to dismiss it. He won't want to do that again. So it seems that the goal argument in *Bridges* would make sense in the Quicklawyer case.

7. Q: Ms. Damion has done a nice job of illustrating that we can take an argument from a prior court opinion and explain why that argument makes sense under the facts of a new case. So, even when the facts and the issues in a new case differ from those in a prior court opinion, you may still be able to use the arguments or rationales from the prior opinion to argue for your client.

    Can anyone else think of a rationale or argument in *Bridges* that might help Mr. Quicklawyer avoid sanctions? Yes, Mr. Packard?

8. A: Well, *Bridges* did say that the purpose or goal behind Rule 11 was not fee shifting. And, if the court awards sanctions in this case, it would be shifting the attorneys' fees incurred by Outofstate to Quicklawyer. So it seems that the argument that Rule 11 is not designed to shift fees can be used to help Quicklawyer avoid sanctions. In addition . . .

In this example, the facts of the hypothetical case create an issue about whether sanctions should be awarded against Quicklawyer under Rule 11. The professor puts a student in the role of the lawyer for Quicklawyer, and asks the student to use the *Bridges* case to make arguments in favor of Quicklawyer (No. 1). The student then explains that because the facts and the issues in *Bridges* are different than those in the Quicklawyer hypothetical, she does not see how the holding in *Bridges* applies to the issue of sanctions in Quicklawyer (No. 2).

The professor then asks the student to focus on the rationales or arguments relied on in the *Bridges* opinion (No. 3). The student then articulates one of the goal arguments relied on in *Bridges* (No. 4). The student then drags and drops that goal argument; that is, the student explains why the goal argument from *Bridges* makes sense when applied to the facts in Quicklawyer (No. 6). Finally, a second student articulates another goal argument relied on in *Bridges* (fee shifting is not the goal of Rule 11) and explains why that goal argument can be used to argue against sanctioning Quicklawyer (No. 8).

Dialogues requiring you to drag and drop arguments from a court opinion to a new case provide you with practice on a critically important skill. In addition, such dialogues should help you appreciate the importance of understanding the arguments in a court opinion as you brief cases in preparation for class. As the dialogue above illustrates, if you do not know the arguments relied on in the *Bridges* opinion, you cannot drag and drop them onto a new case.

II. EXAMPLE #2 — CREATING NEW ARGUMENTS

You are not limited to using court opinions when making arguments for your client. As discussed earlier in Chapter 4, your common sense and/or your specialized knowledge in areas such as quantitative methods, statistics, psychology, history, philosophy, politics, or business may allow you to identify principles, consequences, and analogies that can sometimes be used in legal arguments. As the dialogue below illustrates, professors will sometimes use hypotheticals to require you to create new arguments on behalf of a client.

1. Q: Ms. Kline, let's shift our focus. Assume that you still represent Quicklawyer. I want you to ignore the *Bridges* opinion for the moment. Can you think of any arguments you might make that sanctions should not be awarded against Quicklawyer?

2. A: Well, I'm not sure how to put this, but it seems reasonable for him to have relied on what his client told him. After all, he's trying to build trust and rapport with his client, and he can't do that if he says, in effect, "I need to check out what you've told me before I do anything in reliance on it." That implies that he doesn't trust his client.

3. Q: Are you relying on a principle that lawyers should generally be able to act in reliance on what their clients tell them?

4. A: Well, not always, but generally I think they should be able to do that. If they can't, there might be significant negative consequences.

5. Q: Well, let's examine Ms. Kline's principle and the consequences of applying it in this context. . . .

In this short example, the professor asks a student to go beyond the arguments in the *Bridges* opinion and come up with additional arguments for Quicklawyer. In response, the student, relying on her common sense or her training in psychology, makes an implicit principle argument of her own creation in favor of Quicklawyer (Nos. 2–4).

III. EXAMPLE #3 — ARGUING BOTH WAYS

After exploring the arguments for one party, a professor may ask the class to make a 180-degree turn and practice making arguments on behalf of the opposing party.

1. Q: Mr. Chen, your classmates just made arguments against sanctioning Quicklawyer. Let's assume that your classmates' arguments are sound. For example, let's stipulate that the purpose of Rule 11 is not to shift fees, and if the court declines to award sanctions against Quicklawyer in this case, that decision would be consistent with this "no fee shifting" aspect of Rule 11.

   Now, Mr. Chen, assume that you are the lawyer for Outofstate. In the face of sound arguments against sanctioning Quicklawyer, do you have to close up your briefcase and go home, or can you still make arguments that the court should sanction Quicklawyer?

2. A: I think I can still make arguments that he should be sanctioned. There is no binding precedent directly on point from a higher court. And, as you have told us a million times, sound arguments by one party don't preclude sound arguments for a directly contrary result by the opposing party.

3. Q: I hope I haven't said that a million times, but I take your point, Mr. Chen. So, let's make some arguments that Quicklawyer should be sanctioned. Some of your classmates used the *Bridges* opinion to make arguments against sanctioning Quicklawyer. Can you use the *Bridges* opinion to help you make arguments in favor of sanctioning Quicklawyer?

4. A: I think so. The court in *Bridges* said that sanctions should not be awarded for procedural errors, but can be awarded when a claim is patently unmeritorious. In this case, Quicklawyer didn't make a procedural mistake, he filed a claim that was not justified on the merits because Outofstate's driver just stopped to help and was not involved in the accident. In addition, *Bridges* says that one goal of sanctions under Rule 11 is to deter improper conduct. If plaintiff is sanctioned in this case, it will make it more likely that other lawyers will do a more thorough factual investigation before filing an unmeritorious complaint.

5. Q: Before we examine any responses to those arguments, can you think of any arguments in favor of sanctions that don't rely on the *Bridges* case?

6. A: His client came to see him two days after the accident occurred, so Quicklawyer wasn't facing a statute of limitations problem; he had plenty of time to investigate before filing his complaint. As a general principle, the more time a lawyer has to conduct a factual investigation before filing a complaint, the more thorough we should expect the investigation to be.

7. Q: Okay, that argument seems to make sense. But let's examine it a bit further. Should that principle . . .

There are virtually always sound arguments for resolving an issue both ways. Court opinions may obscure this "sound arguments both ways" phenomenon because such opinions frequently make no mention of legitimate arguments that might support a result directly contrary to that reached by a court. For example, court opinions frequently do not discuss arguments that were advanced by the losing party in the case.[1]

Professors may ask you or a colleague to argue for a 180-degree turn in the face of sound arguments for the other side to provide you with concrete illustrations of the "sound arguments both ways" phenomenon. One hundred and eighty degree turn dialogues also illustrate that as a lawyer you will sometimes acknowledge the validity of one or more of your opponent's arguments. You can do so and still argue that your arguments are more persuasive than your opponent's. Finally, repeated exposures to these dialogues can help to overcome the cognitive discomfort or cognitive dissonance some students experience when they realize that one or more sound arguments are not necessarily dispositive regarding the resolution of an issue.

As this dialogue illustrates, when making argument for a 180-degree turn, you will both drag and drop arguments from a court opinion (Nos. 3–4) and make new arguments of your own creation (Nos. 5–6).

IV. PUTTING YOU IN THE ROLE OF A JUDGE

In the above dialogues, the professor asked students to assume the role a lawyer for one of the parties. Sometimes, however, a professor will pose a hypothetical new case and ask you (or a colleague) to assume the role of a judge. The professor will then ask you what decision you would reach and why. Once you have explained your decision and your rationale for

---

1. Such arguments are, however, sometimes made in a dissenting opinion.

it, the professor may then ask you what were the arguments supporting an opposite result and why you found those arguments unpersuasive. These sorts of classroom dialogues will also illustrate the "sound arguments both ways" phenomenon. And, by placing you in the role of a judge, a professor may also explore the question of how judges reach decisions in the face of competing sound arguments.

V. MAKING ARGUMENTS ABOUT NEW ISSUES — PRACTICE RESPONDING TO EXAM QUESTIONS

Classroom dialogues requiring you to make arguments in hypothetical new cases provide you with opportunities to practice answering exam questions. The hypothetical set of facts in the Quicklawyer example above could have been given to you for the first time on a Civil Procedure exam. The exam could then have asked you to argue that under the facts presented in the Quicklawyer case the lawyer should be sanctioned for violating Rule 11, and to argue that the lawyer should not be sanctioned. Thus, classroom dialogues like those described above provide you with practice at answering exam questions.[2]

---

2. For a discussion of how judges might decide in the face of competing sound arguments, see Chapter 15.

chapter 10

Rule Application Opinions — Classroom Dynamics and Note Taking

I. THE DYNAMICS OF CLASSROOM DIALOGUES AND DISCUSSIONS

For the sake of clarity and ease of illustration, Chapters 6–9 have isolated various subjects that a professor might address in a typical law school classroom. Chapter 6 explored how a professor might help students explore the facts in an opinion, the issue(s) resolved by a court, the arguments a court relied on to resolve each issue, and the legal rules announced in an opinion. Then, Chapter 7 examined how and why professors might ask students to critique a court's arguments. Chapter 8 went on to illustrate likely classroom dialogues concerning a court's holding. Finally, Chapter 9 examined how and why professors might use hypothetical cases to engage students in a consideration of new issues.

Actual classroom discussions, however, will not necessarily complete one subject and then move on to another. For example, a professor may begin a dialogue focused on setting out the court's arguments and, without completely exploring that subject, shift the dialogue to a critique of one of the court's arguments, and then return to setting out the arguments made by the court. Furthermore, a professor will typically not explicitly indicate when these sorts of shifts occur. For example, a professor may <u>not</u> say something like the following: "We've been talking about the arguments discussed by the court in *Bridges* in support of its decision not to award sanctions against plaintiff's counsel. Before we complete that discussion, I'd like to critically examine one of those arguments."

These unlabeled shifts in the focus of classroom dialogues may be designed, at least in part, to mimic the ebb and flow of courtroom exchanges between judges and advocates and give you practice responding to the unexpected shifts in focus that routinely occur in the courtroom. In addition, a professor may quickly shift gears to take advantage of pedagogical opportunities presented by student responses to questions.

Your professors are also unlikely to explore the topics we discuss in Chapters 6 through 9 in the order we have presented them in this book.

For example, a professor may begin one class with a dialogue focused on the facts of a case, and the next class may begin with a critique of an argument in a court's opinion. Finally, the subjects addressed in the classroom will vary from class to class and professor to professor. Some professors may religiously focus the class' attention on the arguments discussed by the court to resolve each issue, whereas other professors may not discuss this topic at all in one class and address it in detail in another. Also, some professors may routinely ask the class to critique a court's arguments, and other professors may seldom do so.

II. TAKING NOTES

There is no single note-taking strategy that works for all students. Some students take close to verbatim notes of what goes on in the classroom and others record relatively little in their class notes. We suggest that, at a minimum, your class notes include the following.

You should record new information about the topics in your case brief in your class notes. Thus, for example, if class discussions clarified your understanding of the legal rules discussed in an opinion, or the arguments relied on by the court, your notes should reflect this clarification. Similarly, if class discussions developed arguments beyond those in the court's opinion, these too should be reflected in your notes. For instance, assume in class discussions you learned about purposes or goals behind the legal rule a court applied that were not mentioned in the court's opinion. You would want to include those purposes and goals in your notes. These purposes and goals will expand your argument repertoire. You may be able to use them to make goal arguments in subsequent classes, on examinations, or in law practice.

You will also want to record the facts of any hypotheticals the professor provided to the class. As you prepare for an exam, you may benefit from reviewing the hypotheticals a professor provided during the course.

part 2

Legal Rule Creation — Creating Broadly Applicable New Legal Rules

Part One focused on rule application opinions; that is, opinions in which the court decides whether the facts of a case satisfy or fail to satisfy one or more legal categories in existing legal rules. Whenever a court applies a legal rule, its decision, which as you now know is called a holding, creates a new legal rule. This new legal rule is, however, generally <u>limited to the facts of the case before the court</u>. Thus, for example, if a court holds that a motor scooter is a vehicle under a statute prohibiting the use of vehicles in a public park, it has created a new legal rule; namely, a motor scooter is a "vehicle" under this statute. This legal rule is limited to the facts of the case. That is, the rule controls the outcome in future cases involving motor scooters, but does not control the outcome in cases that do not involve motor scooters. For instance, a holding that a motor scooter is a vehicle would not resolve an issue of whether a defendant who used a skateboard in a park had violated the rule governing the use of vehicles in a park.[1]

Applying existing rules to a set of facts, however, is not the only way in which courts create new legal rules. Some court opinions create or adopt broadly applicable new legal rules that go <u>beyond the facts of the case before the court</u>. These opinions are typically focused on what the legal rule should be. We refer to these "what should the legal rule be" opinions as "rule creation opinions." Three common types of rule creation opinions are described below.

---

1. The case that holds that a motor scooter is a "vehicle" might, of course, be used to make an argument by analogy in a case involving a skateboard.

I. NEW RULES DEFINING AN EXISTING LEGAL CATEGORY

As you know from reading Part One, legal rules are composed of legal categories. Court opinions sometimes create broadly applicable new legal rules by **defining, or elaborating on the meaning of, an existing legal category.** For example, assume that a defendant riding a bicycle in a public park in the State of Ultimate Clarity is charged with violating the now-familiar "no vehicles in the park" statute. The defendant admits that he was riding his bicycle in a public park, but contends that a bicycle is not a vehicle. Assume that the trial court finds the defendant/bicycle rider guilty. On appeal, the highest appellate court in the State of Ultimate Clarity decides as follows:

> We hold that a "vehicle" under this statute includes **any mechanical device that people commonly use for transportation.** A bicycle obviously meets this definition, it is therefore a vehicle, and we uphold the defendant's conviction.

This holding does more than just resolve the question of whether a bicycle is a vehicle. The holding also creates a new, broadly applicable rule that defines the existing legal category "vehicle" in the statute. This new rule is: **A vehicle in this statute means any mechanical device that people commonly use for transportation.** This new legal rule is a rule of broad application because it is not limited to future cases involving bicycles; it applies to all future cases in the State of Ultimate Clarity interpreting "vehicle" under this statute.

Consider another example. Assume that the legislature in the State of Bliss passes a statute defining the crime of attempt as follows:

> An act, done with intent to commit a crime, and tending but failing to effect its commission, is an attempt to commit that crime.

When resolving the case of *State v. Lay* arising under this statute, the highest court in the State of Bliss holds that the legal category "tending but failing to effect its commission" in the above attempt statute is satisfied whenever the acts of a defendant are as follows:

> **So near to the accomplishment of the crime that in all reasonable probability the crime itself would have been committed, but for timely interference.**

Such a holding creates a broadly applicable new legal rule defining the existing legal category "tending but failing to effect its commission." This new legal rule goes beyond the facts of *State v. Lay* (whatever those facts may be) and applies to all future cases in the State of Bliss interpreting the "tending but failing to effect its commission" category in the attempt statute.

Courts create new rules defining existing legal categories for at least two reasons. First, defining an existing legal category frequently increases the probability that similar cases will have similar outcomes. For example, under the above attempt statute, an act "tending to effect the commission of a crime" may subject a defendant to criminal liability for attempt. The word "tending" is relatively broad and indefinite, however. Consequently, it is relatively easy for different judges or juries to disagree about whether a defendant's conduct satisfies or fails to satisfy that legal category. As a result, if in two separate cases two defendants engage in essentially the same conduct, one might be convicted of an attempt whereas the other might be found not guilty. When courts create a new rule providing a more **precise definition** of an existing legal category, it increases the likelihood that like cases will be treated alike, and thus two defendants engaged in essentially the same conduct are more likely to be subject to the same verdict at trial.

Second, the added precision provided by a legal rule defining an existing legal category frequently increases people's ability to predict the outcome of the application of legal rules. This facilitates settlement of litigation and allows people to more accurately weigh the costs and benefits of a particular course of action as they plan their affairs.

II. CHANGING THE EXISTING LEGAL RULES

Rule creation opinions can sometimes change (or refuse to change) the existing legal rules.[2] For instance, assume that prior cases from the highest court in a State have held that an owner of land has no duty to protect adjacent property from dangers created by natural conditions. The highest court in that State can hold that that legal rule is no longer valid and that henceforth landowners do have a duty to protect adjacent property from dangers resulting from natural conditions.[3] This holding creates a broadly applicable new legal rule that would apply to all future cases involving a landowner's duty to protect adjacent property.

III. RESOLVING RULE CONFLICTS IN THE LOWER COURTS

Rule creation opinions can also resolve conflicts in lower court rulings. For example, assume that one lower state court has announced a rule that

---

2. In at least one of your first-year courses, you will consider the question of when and why courts are permitted to change existing legal rules.

3. See *Sprecher v. Adamson Cos.*, 30 Cal. 3d 358 (1981).

a contract for the adoption of an as yet unborn child is unenforceable, and another lower court in the same state has adopted a contrary rule. A higher state court can clarify the situation by holding that one of the lower courts' holdings is correct. The holding will then apply to all future cases in the state involving contracts for the adoption of unborn children.

IV. "SHOULD THE COURT CREATE A NEW RULE" CONSTITUTES AN "ISSUE"

As you know from reading Part One, in class your professor will routinely ask you to identify the "issue" or "issues" faced by the court writing an opinion. In rule creation opinions, the **"issue"** faced by courts is what, if any, new broadly applicable legal rule that goes <u>beyond the facts of the case before the court</u> should be created.

V. ISSUES INVOLVING WHAT, IF ANY, NEW LEGAL RULE SHOULD BE CREATED ARE RESOLVED BY MAKING ARGUMENTS

In rule creation opinions, courts routinely rely on the same types of arguments discussed in Chapter 4 to explain or justify their decision to create a new legal rule of broad applicability. For example, assume once again that the legislature in the State of Bliss passes a statute defining the crime of attempt as follows:

> An act, done with intent to commit a crime, and tending but failing to effect its commission, is an attempt to commit that crime.

In the case of *State v. Lay* arising under this statute, the highest court in the State of Bliss holds that the legal category "tending but failing to effect its commission" in the above attempt statute is satisfied whenever the acts of a defendant are as follows:

> So near to the accomplishment of the crime that in all reasonable probability the crime itself would have been committed, but for timely interference.

The court might use one or more of the following arguments to justify its creation of this broadly applicable new legal rule.

- One can **infer** from the legislative history of the statute that the legislature in the State of Bliss intended the statute to apply only to conduct that came very close to the commission of a crime. Therefore, the new rule is consistent with the **goal** behind the statute.

- The new rule will provide guidance to trial courts, prosecutors, and defense attorneys about the type of conduct that constitutes an attempt in future cases arising under the statute. This guidance will increase the likelihood that like cases will be treated alike. This is a positive **consequence** of creating the new rule.

- The new rule is consistent with the results in the vast majority of the cases already decided under this statute. Thus, the new rule is consistent with the **principle** that newly created legal rules should generally be consistent with prior court opinions.

- The new rule is identical to the rule adopted in several other states. Thus, there is **non-binding precedent** to support the new rule.

Because courts routinely rely on the same types of arguments discussed in Chapter 4 in rule creation opinions, you will not need to learn a new argument typology in order to understand many of the arguments in these sorts of opinions.

VI. CONCLUSION

In the next two chapters, we consider how you might prepare for class when reading rule creation opinions (Chapter 11), and examine and illustrate how your preparation can help you understand some of the typical subjects discussed when analyzing rule creation opinions in the classroom (Chapter 12). In Chapter 13 we examine an opinion that resolves issues related to **both** rule application and rule creation.

Reading Rule Creation Opinions in Preparation for Class — Preparing a Case "Brief"

This chapter sets out the opinion in *Barker v. Lull Engineering*, an example of a rule creation opinion you might be asked to read in your Torts class. Next, the chapter explores how you might prepare for class when reading a rule creation opinion.

As the *Barker* opinion illustrates, reading rule creation opinions in preparation for class can be quite time consuming because courts sometimes go to considerable lengths to explain their reasons for creating a new rule.

After discussing how you might prepare for class, the chapter concludes with an illustrative example of a case brief in *Barker*. As you know from Chapter 5, your case brief is the written preparation you will take into the classroom.

I. *BARKER V. LULL ENGINEERING* 20 CAL. 3D 413 CALIFORNIA SUPREME COURT (1978)

A. Background Information

At the time of the court's opinion in *Barker*, it was well established under California law that a manufacturer was strictly liable in tort for injuries proximately caused by its defective products, and that a product could be defective either in its manufacture or in its design.

Plaintiff Ray Barker was injured at a construction site while operating a high-lift loader manufactured by defendant Lull Engineering Co. Plaintiff's lawsuit alleged that the high-lift loader was defectively designed and that the defect in design proximately caused plaintiff's injuries. In the trial court, one of the issues was whether the legal category "defect in design" should be further defined for the jury. The trial judge decided that "defect in design" should be further defined to mean that the design made the product "unreasonably dangerous" and instructed the jury to that effect. The jury returned a verdict for defendant Lull Engineering and the plaintiff appealed.

On appeal, the main issue before the California Supreme Court was how should "design defect" be defined.

B. The Court's Opinion in *Barker v. Lull Engineering*

Tobriner, Acting C. J.

... As we explain in more detail below, we have concluded ... that a product is defective in design either (1) if the product has failed to perform as safely as an ordinary consumer would expect when used in an intended or reasonably foreseeable manner, or (2) if, in light of the relevant factors discussed below, the benefits of the challenged design do not outweigh the risk of danger inherent in such design. In addition, we explain how the burden of proof with respect to the latter "risk-benefit" standard should be allocated.

This dual standard for design defect assures an injured plaintiff protection from products that either fall below ordinary consumer expectations as to safety, or that, on balance, are not as safely designed as they should be. At the same time, the standard permits a manufacturer who has marketed a product which satisfies ordinary consumer expectations to demonstrate the relative complexity of design decisions and the trade-offs that are frequently required in the adoption of alternative designs. Finally, this test reflects our continued adherence to the principle that, in a product liability action, the trier of fact must focus on the *product*, not on the *manufacturer's conduct*, and that the plaintiff need not prove that the manufacturer acted unreasonably or negligently in order to prevail in such an action.

[Fact of the Case]

Plaintiff Barker sustained serious injuries as a result of an accident which occurred while he was operating a Lull High-Lift Loader at a construction site. The loader, manufactured in 1967, is a piece of heavy construction equipment designed to lift loads of up to 5,000 pounds to a maximum height of 32 feet. ... The loader is designed so that the load can be kept level even when the loader is being operated on sloping terrain. The leveling of the load is controlled by a lever located near the steering column, and positioned between the operator's legs. The lever is equipped with a manual lock that can be engaged to prevent accidental slipping of the load level during lifting.

The loader was not equipped with seat belts or a roll bar. A wire and pipe cage over the driver's seat afforded the driver some protection from falling objects. The cab of the loader was located at least nine feet behind the lifting forks.

On the day of the accident the regular operator of the loader, Bill Dalton, did not report for work, and plaintiff, who had received only limited instruction on the operation of the loader from Dalton and who had operated the loader on only a few occasions, was assigned to run the loader in Dalton's place. The accident occurred while plaintiff was attempting to lift a load of lumber to a height of approximately 18 to 20 feet and to place the load on the second story of a building under construction. The lift was a particularly difficult one because the terrain on which the loader rested sloped sharply in several directions.

Witnesses testified that plaintiff approached the structure with the loader, leveled the forks to compensate for the sloping ground and lifted the load to a height variously estimated between 10 and 18 feet. During the course of the lift plaintiff felt some vibration, and, when it appeared to several coworkers that the load was beginning to tip, the workers shouted to plaintiff to jump from the loader. Plaintiff heeded these warnings and leaped from the loader, but while scrambling away he was struck by a piece of falling lumber and suffered serious injury.

[Discussion Regarding Design Defect]

Plaintiff principally contends that the trial court committed prejudicial error in instructing the jury "that strict liability for a defect in design of a product is based on a finding that the product was unreasonably dangerous for its intended use. . . ." Plaintiff maintains that this instruction conflicts directly with this court's decision in *Cronin*, decided subsequently to the instant trial, and mandates a reversal of the judgment. . . .

After undertaking a thorough review of the origins and development of both California product liability doctrine and the Restatement's "unreasonably dangerous" criterion [in *Cronin*], we . . . [decided] . . . "that to require an injured plaintiff to prove not only that the product contained a defect but also that such defect made the product unreasonably dangerous to the user or consumer would place a considerably greater burden upon him than that articulated in *Greenman* [v. *Yuba Power Products, Inc.* (1963) 59 Cal. 2d 57 (27 Cal. Rptr. 697, 377 P.2d 897, 13 A.L.R. 3d 1049), . . .

Thus, our rejection of the use of the "unreasonably dangerous" terminology in *Cronin* rested in part on a concern that a jury might interpret such an instruction, as the Restatement draftsman had indeed intended, as shielding a defendant from liability so long as the product did not fall below the ordinary consumer's expectations as to the product's safety. . . .

[I]n *Cronin* itself we expressly stated that our holding applied to design defects as well as to manufacturing defects (8 Cal. 3d at pp. 134–135), and in *Henderson v. Harnischfeger Corp.* (1974) 12 Cal. 3d 663, 670 [117 Cal. Rptr. 1, 527 P.2d 353], we subsequently confirmed the impropriety of instructing a jury in the language of the "unreasonably dangerous" standard in a design defect case. (See also *Foglio v. Western Auto Supply* (1976) 56 Cal. App. 3d 470, 475 [128 Cal. Rptr. 545].) [FN8] Consequently, we conclude that the design defect instruction given in the instant case was erroneous. . . .

As this court has recognized on numerous occasions, the term defect as utilized in the strict liability context is neither self-defining nor susceptible to a single definition applicable in all contexts. . . . Resort to the numerous product liability precedents in California demonstrates that the defect or defectiveness concept has embraced a great variety of injury-producing deficiencies . . . Commentators have pointed out that in view of the diversity of product deficiencies to which the defect rubric has been applied, an instruction which requires a plaintiff to prove the existence of a product defect, but which fails to elaborate on the meaning of defect in a particular context, may in some situations prove more misleading than helpful. . . .

[O]ur cases establish that a product may be found defective in design if the plaintiff demonstrates that the product failed to perform as safely as an ordinary consumer would expect when used in an intended or reasonably foreseeable manner. This initial standard, somewhat analogous to the Uniform Commercial Code's warranty of fitness and merchantability (Cal. U. Com. Code, § 2314), reflects the warranty heritage upon which California product liability doctrine in part rests. As we noted in *Greenman*, "implicit in [a product's] presence on the market . . . [is] a representation that it [will] safely do the jobs for which it was built." (59 Cal. 2d at p. 64.) When a product fails to satisfy such ordinary consumer expectations as to safety in its intended or reasonably foreseeable operation, a manufacturer is strictly liable for resulting injuries. (*Greenman, supra* . . . Under this standard, an injured plaintiff will frequently be able to demonstrate the defectiveness of a product by resorting to circumstantial evidence, even when the accident itself precludes identification of the specific defect at fault. . . .

[T]he expectations of the ordinary consumer cannot be viewed as the exclusive yardstick for evaluating design defectiveness because "[i]n many situations . . . the consumer would not know what to expect, because he would have no idea how safe the product could be made." (Wade, *On the Nature of Strict Tort Liability for Products, supra*, 44 Miss. L.J. 825, 829) Numerous California decisions have implicitly recognized this fact and have made clear, through varying linguistic formulations, that a product may be found defective in design, even if it satisfies ordinary consumer expectations, if through hindsight the jury determines that the product's design embodies "excessive preventable danger," or, in other words, if the jury finds that the risk of danger inherent in the challenged design outweighs the benefits of such design. (E.g., *Self v. General Motors Corp., supra*, 42 Cal. App. 3d at p. 6 . . .

A review of past cases indicates that in evaluating the adequacy of a product's design pursuant to this latter standard, a jury may consider, among other relevant factors, the gravity of the danger posed by the challenged design, the likelihood that such danger would occur, the mechanical feasibility of a safer alternative design, the financial cost of an improved design, and the adverse consequences to the product and to the consumer that would result from an alternative design. (See, e.g., *Horn v. General Motors Corp.* (1976) 17 Cal. 3d 359, 367 [131 Cal. Rptr. 78, 551 P.2d 398]; . . .

[Discussion Regarding Burden of Proof]

Although our cases have thus recognized a variety of considerations that may be relevant to the determination of the adequacy of a product's design, past authorities have generally not devoted much attention to the appropriate allocation of the burden of proof with respect to these matters. . . . The allocation of such burden is particularly significant in this context inasmuch as this court's product liability decisions, from *Greenman* to *Cronin*, have repeatedly emphasized that one of the principal purposes behind the strict product liability doctrine is to relieve an injured plaintiff of many of the onerous evidentiary burdens inherent in a negligence cause of action. Because most of the evidentiary matters which may be relevant to the determination of the adequacy of a product's design under the "risk-benefit" standard — e.g., the feasibility and cost of alternative designs — are similar to issues typically presented in a negligent design case and involve technical matters peculiarly within the knowledge of the manufacturer, we conclude that once the plaintiff makes a prima facie showing that the injury was proximately caused by the product's design, the burden should appropriately shift to the defendant to prove, in light of the relevant factors, that the product is not defective. Moreover, inasmuch as this conclusion flows from our determination that the fundamental public policies embraced in *Greenman* dictate that a manufacturer who seeks to escape liability for an injury proximately caused by its product's design on a risk-benefit theory should bear the burden of persuading the trier of fact that its product should not be judged defective, the defendant's burden is one affecting the burden of proof, rather than simply the burden of producing evidence. . . .)

[Further Elaboration On Meaning of Design Defect & The Burden of Proof]

Thus, to reiterate, a product may be found defective in design, so as to subject a manufacturer to strict liability for resulting injuries, under either of two alternative tests. First, a product may be found defective in design if the plaintiff establishes that the product failed to perform as safely as an ordinary consumer would expect when used in an intended or reasonably foreseeable manner. Second, a product may alternatively be found defective in design if the plaintiff demonstrates that the product's design proximately caused his injury and the defendant fails to establish, in light of the relevant factors, that, on balance, the benefits of the challenged design outweigh the risk of danger inherent in such design.

Although past California decisions have not explicitly articulated the two-pronged definition of design defect which we have elaborated above, other jurisdictions have adopted a somewhat similar, though not identical, dual approach in attempting to devise instructions to guide the jury in design defect cases. (See, e.g., *Henderson v. Ford Motor Co.* (Tex. 1974) 519 S.W.2d 87, 92 . . . As we have indicated, we believe that the test for defective design set out above is appropriate in light of the rationale and limits of the strict liability doctrine, for it subjects a manufacturer to liability whenever there is something "wrong" with a product's design — either because the product fails to meet ordinary consumer expectations as to safety or because, on balance, the design is not as safe as it should be — while stopping short of making the manufacturer an insurer for all injuries which may result from the use of its product. This test, moreover, explicitly focuses the trier of fact's attention on the adequacy of the product itself, rather than on the manufacturer's conduct, and places the burden on the manufacturer, rather than the plaintiff, to establish that because of the complexity of, and trade-offs implicit in, the design process, an injury-producing product should nevertheless not be found defective.

[Conclusion]

The technological revolution has created a society that contains dangers to the individual never before contemplated. The individual must face the threat to life and limb not only from the car on the street or highway but from a massive array of hazardous mechanisms and products. The radical change from a comparatively safe, largely agricultural, society to this industrial unsafe one has been reflected in the decisions that formerly tied liability to the fault of a tortfeasor but now are more concerned with the safety of the individual who suffers the loss. As Dean Keeton has written, "The change in the substantive law as regards the liability of makers of products and other sellers in the marketing chain has been from fault to defect. The plaintiff is no longer required to impugn the maker, but he is required to impugn the product." (Keeton, *Product Liability and the Meaning of Defect* (1973) 5 St. Mary's L.J. 30, 33)

If a jury in determining liability for a defect in design is instructed only that it should decide whether or not there is "a defective design," it may reach to the extreme conclusion that the plaintiff, having suffered injury, should without further showing, recover; on the other hand, it may go to the opposite extreme and conclude that because the product matches the intended design the plaintiff, under no conceivable circumstance, could recover. The submitted definition eschews both extremes and attempts a balanced approach.

We hold that a trial judge may properly instruct the jury that a product is defective in design (1) if the plaintiff demonstrates that the product failed to perform as safely as an ordinary consumer would expect when used in an intended or reasonably foreseeable manner, or (2) if the plaintiff proves that the product's design proximately caused his injury and the defendant fails to prove, in light of the relevant factors discussed above, that on balance the benefits of the challenged design outweigh the risk of danger inherent in such design.

Because the jury may have interpreted the erroneous instruction given in the instant case as requiring plaintiff to prove that the high-lift loader was ultrahazardous or more dangerous than the average consumer contemplated . . . we cannot find that the error was harmless on the facts of this case. [The Court then sent the case back to the trial court for a retrial using the proper jury instruction defining design defect.]

The judgment in favor of defendants is reversed.

II. PREPARING FOR CLASS IN *BARKER V. LULL ENGINEERING*

As you read a rule creation opinion in preparation for class, you will benefit from identifying each of the following:

- The new rule(s) created or adopted in the opinion. (The "issue" in a rule creation opinion is what new rule(s), if any, should be created or adopted.)

- The arguments relied on by the court to create or adopt the new rule.

- Any legal rule alternatives rejected by the opinion.

- A summary of the facts in the opinion.

The remainder of this section identifies these four topics in the *Barker* opinion and explains how identifying them can help you to understand classroom dialogues and discussions, to answer law school exam questions, and to succeed in the practice of law.

A. The New Legal Rule Created in *Barker v. Lull Engineering*

You might reasonably see the court's opinion in *Barker* as creating a single new legal rule that defines the existing legal category of "defect in design."[4] This new legal rule might be stated as follows:

In a products liability case, "defect in design" means <u>either</u> that:

Definition A

A product has failed to perform as safely as an ordinary consumer would expect when used in an intended or reasonably foreseeable manner and the failure is the proximate cause of plaintiff's injury.

or

Definition B

Plaintiff demonstrates that the product's design proximately caused his injury and the defendant fails to establish in light of the relevant factors that, on balance, the benefits of the challenged design outweigh the risk of danger inherent in such design.

When determining whether the benefits outweigh the risks, among other relevant factors, the trier of fact may consider the following factors:

- the gravity of the danger posed by the challenged design
- the likelihood that such danger would occur
- the mechanical feasibility of a safer alternative design
- the financial cost of an improved design
- the adverse consequences to the product that would result from an alternative design
- the adverse consequences to the consumer that would result from an alternative design

Because the issue in a rule creation opinion is what legal rule, if any, should the court create or adopt, the issue in *Barker* is how

---

4. We say that you "might reasonably see" the rule in *Barker* this way because there is frequently more than one reasonable way to characterize the rule or rules created by a court. You might, for example, see *Barker* as creating one new rule defining "defect in design" and assigning to the defendant the obligation to prove that the benefits of the challenged design outweigh the risks. Alternatively, you might see the opinion as creating two new rules; one rule defining "defect in design" and one rule relating to the allocation of the burden of proof regarding the obligation to prove that the benefits of the challenged design outweigh the risks.

"design defect" should be defined. When you identify the new legal rule created in the opinion, you have determined how the court resolved the issue.

Of course, the new legal rules created in court opinions, like all legal rules, are typically composed of one of more legal categories. For example, definition A above might be seen as containing the following legal categories: **A "product" (Category 1) has "failed to perform as safely as an ordinary consumer would expect" (Category 2) when "used in an intended manner" (Category 3) or "reasonably foreseeable manner" (Category 4) and the "failure is the proximate cause of plaintiff's injury" (Category 5).**

1. The Benefits of Identifying the New Legal Rule

In class, your professors will routinely ask you or a classmate questions about the new legal rule created in the court's opinion. For example, a professor may ask you or a colleague questions such as, "Just what was the rule announced by the court in *Barker*?" and "What rule did the court articulate regarding the shifting of the burden of proof?" Identifying the new rule as you prepare for class will help you to understand and participate in these sorts of classroom dialogues.

Identifying the new rule created in an opinion will also help you on law school exams. In one type of typical exam question, you will be given a set of facts, but you will not be given the legal rule(s) that apply to that set of facts. Instead, you will need to know the applicable legal rule and also be able to break the rule into categories and decide if the facts on the exam satisfy each category. The legal rule(s) you typically need to know for an exam include (but are not limited to) the legal rules created or adopted by courts in the rule creation opinions you read for class.

Other types of law school exam questions will also require you to know the legal rule adopted or created in a court opinion. Consider the following possible law school examination question.

> The rule adopted in *Barker v. Lull Engineering* unduly favors plaintiffs. Comment.

You will be better able to respond to this exam question if you know the rules created in the *Barker* opinion.

In short, when you identify the new rules created in rule creation opinions, you are preparing for law school exams.

As you prepare for class, you will typically want to identify the full text of any new rule created in a rule creation opinion. If you need to apply that rule to the facts on a law school examination, vague shorthand references to the rule will not suffice. For example, assume as you prepared for class you identified the legal rule in *Barker* as follows: "A product can be defectively designed if it fails to meet consumer expectations or the benefits of the design outweigh the risks." Although this shorthand may arguably capture the essence of the rule, it will not suffice for the category-by-category analysis required on many law school examinations. For example, reasonable people might differ about whether the facts on the examination satisfy or fail to satisfy the legal category **"reasonably foreseeable use"** in the rule created in *Barker*, but the above shorthand statement of the rule does not include this legal category. As a result, if you were using the shorthand statement on an exam, you might miss an issue relating to **"reasonably foreseeable use"** and lose precious points.

Identifying the new rules in rule creation opinions can also help you in law practice. The rules you learn as you read rule creation opinions in law school may apply to the problems clients present to you in law practice. In addition, in practice (or if you have a legal job during law school) you will frequently be required to read opinions you did not read in law school and identify the legal rules created in those opinions.

2. Tips for Identifying a New Legal Rule

In many rule creation opinions, identifying a new legal rule will be relatively easy. A court opinion will frequently do the work for you by explicitly setting out the new legal rule. In *Barker*, for example, the court might have said something like: "We adopt the following new definition of 'design defect' in California: A product is defective in design when. . . ."

When a rule creation opinion does not clearly identify a new legal rule, if you are having difficulty identifying it, try one or more of the following approaches:

- Look for language in the opinion indicating that the court is **defining or clarifying the meaning of** a preexisting legal category.

- Look for language in the opinion describing a **test,** or **conduct that will be required in the future** to meet a legal standard.

- Look for **factors** that will be considered in future cases to determine whether or not a legal standard has been met.

These prompts should help you to identify a new rule created by the court in a rule creation opinion.

B. The Arguments Relied on by the Court in *Barker v. Lull Engineering* to Justify Creating the New Legal Rule

The arguments relied on by the court in *Barker* to justify its new rule defining "design defect" might[5] be set out as follows:

Definition A

Arguments Supporting Definition A

(1) The *Cronin* opinion said that it's holding that a product must meet ordinary consumer expectations applied to <u>both</u> design defects and manufacturing defects. (This might be seen as an argument from precedent or by analogy.)

(2) The "consumer expectations" standard for design defect is established by "our cases." (This might be seen as an argument from precedent or by analogy.)

(3) The "warranty heritage" of the rule of strict products liability, and a prior case (*Greenman*), indicate that one of the purposes of strict products liability is to make sure that a product is fit for its intended use. "[I]mplicit in [a product's] presence on the market . . . [is] a representation that it [will] safely do the jobs for which it was built." (This might be seen as a goal argument, i.e. the new rule created by the court will increase the likelihood that products will be fit for an intended use. Alternatively this argument might be seen as a combination of a goal argument and an argument by analogy from the prior case.)

Definition B

Arguments Supporting Definition B

(1) The expectations of the ordinary consumer cannot be viewed as an exclusive yardstick for design defect because consumers may not know how safe a product could be made. Therefore, if a product's design embodies "excessive preventable danger," it should be considered defective. (This might be seen as a consequences argument. Definition B will encourage manufacturers to eliminate excess preventable dangers in their products; a positive consequence. Alternatively, this argument might be seen as a principle argument: Products should not be placed on the market if the design results in excessive preventable danger.)

---

5. Again, we say "might" be set out because reasonable lawyers, judges, law professors, and law students can almost always reasonably disagree about how to characterize the arguments relied on by a court.

(2) It gives a manufacturer an opportunity to avoid liability by demonstrating design trade-offs involved when selecting among design alternatives; manufacturers are not insurers. (This might be seen as a consequences argument; providing this opportunity to manufacturers is a positive consequence. It might also be seen as a principle argument; that is, manufacturers should not be treated as insurers.)

(3) It is consistent with the principle that a product rather than a manufacturer's conduct should be the focus of a trier of fact's inquiry. This might not be the focus if the unreasonably dangerous standard were adopted. (This might be seen as a principle argument. It might also be seen as a consequences argument; that is, the new rule will encourage the trier of fact to examine the product and not the manufacturer's conduct, and that is a positive consequence.)

(4) Numerous cases, with "varying linguistic formulations," have recognized a similar rule. (This might be seen as an argument from precedent or by analogy.)

(5) One purpose of strict products liability was to relieve the plaintiff of the onerous burden of proof in a negligence cause of action. This rule does that. (This might be seen as a goal or consequences argument.)

(6) Usually defendants have access to most of the information relevant to the factors to be considered under the risk/benefit prong of the definition of design defect. Because defendants generally have the relevant information, and one purpose of strict product liability was to relieve the plaintiff of the onerous burden of proof in a negligence cause of action, it seems appropriate to shift the burden of proof under this test. (This might be seen as a combination of a goal and a principle argument. One of the goals of strict products liability is to relieve plaintiff of a burdensome burden of proof and as a general principle it is fair to place the burden of proof on the party with easy access to most of the relevant evidence.)

(7) Other cases involving design defects have indicated that these are the relevant factors. (This might be seen as an argument from precedent or by analogy.)

Argument Supporting Both Definitions A and B

Other jurisdictions have adopted a similar two-pronged approach. (This might be seen as an argument from precedent or by analogy.)

1. The Benefits of Identifying Arguments Relied on by the Court

Your professors will routinely ask you or a classmate to articulate the court's reasons or justifications for creating or adopting a new legal rule. These reasons or justifications are the arguments relied on by the court. Identifying these arguments as you prepare for class will help you to understand and participate in these sorts of classroom dialogues.

If you have identified each of the court's arguments as you prepare for class, it may then be easier for you to spot potential weaknesses or rebuttals to each argument. Identifying weaknesses in, and rebuttals to, arguments are critical skills in law practice. In the classroom, a professor will frequently allow you to practice these skills by asking you or a colleague to critique the arguments relied on by a court to create a new legal rule.

To perform well on many law school exams and as a lawyer in practice, you may be required to make arguments about the legal rule that should be adopted by a court, a legislature, or another rule-making body. For example, assume that on a law school examination you are presented with the following question:

> You are the law clerk for an appellate judge in the great State of Equipoise. The law of the State of Equipoise provides that manufactures are strictly liable for injuries proximately caused by "design defects" in their products. The term "design defect" has not been further defined by any of the appellate courts in the State of Equipoise. The judge has a case before her involving an allegedly defectively designed product and she is considering whether to further define the term "design defect" for the trial courts in her state. The judge has asked you to write her a memo setting forth:
>
> 1) The arguments for and against further defining the term "design defect."
>
> 2) Assuming the term is to be further defined, the arguments for and against using the definition established by the *Barker v. Lull Engineering* case.

You will be better able to answer this sort of "what should the legal rule be" type of question on an examination if you have identified the arguments the court made in *Barker*. Furthermore, if you consistently identify the arguments relied on by a court to create new legal rules as you prepare for your classes, you are likely to gain a better sense of how to articulate these sorts of arguments on examinations and in practice.

2. Tips for Identifying the Court's Arguments

The arguments a court relies on for creating a new legal rule are sometimes easy to identify. The opinion may say something like, "We adopt this rule for the following three reasons" and then neatly summarize the arguments relied on by the court. In many rule creation opinions, however, the court's arguments will **not** be set out in a separate section of the opinion or under a heading such as, "Arguments and Rationales Justifying Our Creation of the New Rule." In addition, as is the case in the *Barker* opinion, a court frequently considers multiple alternatives before deciding on a new legal rule. The arguments for and against each of these multiple alternatives are often dispersed throughout the opinion.

If you are having difficulties identifying the court's arguments, you may find one or more of the following approaches helpful:

- Does the court say anything about the goals or purposes behind preexisting legal rules? Does the court say anything about whether the new rule(s) it creates would further or undermine those goals? Answering these questions may help to identify goal arguments.

- Does the court indicate that the new rule(s) will lead to any positive consequences or avoid negative ones? Does the court indicate that the rule(s) will change the way people will behave in the future? Answering these questions may help to identify consequences arguments.

- Does the court make a normative statement about how things should usually happen, how texts should be interpreted, or how people should usually behave? Does the court make any normative criticisms of anyone's conduct? Answering these questions may help to identify principle arguments.

- Does the court refer to other court decisions that have adopted the same or similar legal rule(s)? Answering these questions may help to identify precedent arguments and arguments by analogy.

- Does the court explain why it believes people will change their behavior in response to the new rule(s) that are created or clarified? Answering this question may help to identify inference arguments.

C. Legal Rule Alternatives Considered and Rejected by the Court — Paths Not Taken

When an opinion creates a new legal rule, the opinion will also sometimes explicitly reject proposed alternative legal rules. In *Barker*, for example, the court explicitly rejected the approach of leaving a design defect undefined. On an exam or in the classroom, a professor will sometimes ask about proposed legal rule alternatives rejected by a court and the reasons for a court's rejection. Consequently, as you prepare for class you may want to identify any rejected alternatives and the arguments advanced by the court to support its rejection. Doing so may help you answer exam questions or understand classroom dialogues addressed to these topics. In *Barker*, for example, as you prepare for class you might identify the following:

The "Leave Design Defect Undefined" Alternative.

Argument Against This Alternative

The Court indicates that "design defect" is a very broad term, applying to a wide range of circumstances, with no precise, generally accepted definition. If design defect were left undefined, some triers of fact might go to the "extreme" of granting recovery whenever the defect caused an injury, while other juries might go to the other "extreme" and "conclude that because the product matches the intended design" no recovery is possible. These two extreme outcomes would violate the generally accepted legal principle that like cases should be treated alike.

D. A Summary of the Facts of the Case

You know from reading Chapter 5 that the facts of a case typically include both the pre-litigation facts (the events that occurred before the courts became involved) and the post-litigation facts (the events that occurred after the courts became involved). In an opinion like *Barker*, in which the court creates a new legal rule but does not apply the newly created rule, you can sometimes understand the new legal rule and the arguments supporting the court's decision even if you have only a superficial understanding of the facts of the case. For example, you could understand the new legal rule created in *Barker* even if you did not understand exactly how the high-lift loader was designed or how the design of the loader contributed to plaintiff's injury.

Nevertheless, you will usually benefit by knowing the basic facts of the case in rule creation opinions, for at least two reasons. First, a professor may ask you about the pre-litigation and/or the post-litigation facts of a case creating a new legal rule. In addition, a professor may ask you to apply the new rules announced in a case to the pre-litigation facts of that case. In *Barker*, for example, the professor may ask you or a colleague to argue that the high-lift loader used by Barker was or was not defective under the new rules announced in the *Barker* court's opinion. This exercise would give you practice breaking down the rules announced in *Barker* into legal categories, proceeding category by category through the rule, and making arguments to resolve the issues created by the application of the new rule. You will have difficulty participating in this exercise if you do not know the facts of the case.

Second, many law school exam questions contain a statement of facts. Many exam questions will not tell you the specific legal rules that apply to those facts, however. Consequently, you will routinely be required to determine the legal rules that apply to the facts on an exam question before you can answer the question. Understanding the facts of each case that you read for class will help you make that determination. If you know the facts of the *Barker* case, for example, you may realize that they are similar or analogous to the facts on an exam question. As a result, you may realize that the facts on the exam may trigger the application of the legal rules in *Barker*.

III. PRESERVING YOUR PREPARATION — AN ILLUSTRATIVE EXAMPLE OF A CASE BRIEF IN *BARKER V. LULL ENGINEERING*

This chapter has discussed why you may benefit from identifying the new rule(s) created by the court, the arguments supporting the creation of the new rule(s), the legal rule alternative(s) rejected by the court, and the facts of the case as you read a rule creation opinion in preparation for class. As you identify these matters, you should preserve them in a manner that allows you ready access to them in class. You may decide to record some or all of these matters on paper or in a computer. Alternatively, you may decide to simply identify some or all of these matters with annotations, marginal notes, highlighting, or other designations directly in your textbook (this is usually referred to as "book briefing"). For example, you might indicate "first issue" in the margin of your textbook and highlight or underscore the court's arguments related to the resolution of that issue.

If you choose to write out your entire case brief in *Barker*, it might look something like the following:

Barker Brief

First Issue — What new rule should be created to define the legal category "design defect." The court adopted the following definition:

In a products liability case, "defect in design" means either that:

Definition A — A product has failed to perform as safely as an ordinary consumer would expect when used in an intended or reasonably foreseeable manner and the failure is the proximate cause of plaintiff's injury.

or

Definition B — Plaintiff demonstrates that the product's design proximately caused his injury and the defendant fails to establish in light of the relevant factors that, on balance, the benefits of the challenged design outweigh the risk of danger inherent in such design.

When determining whether the benefits outweigh the risks, among other relevant factors, the trier of fact may consider the following factors:

> (1) the gravity of the danger posed by the challenged design; (2) the likelihood that such danger would occur; (3) the mechanical feasibility of a safer alternative design; (4) the financial cost of an improved design; (5) the adverse consequences to the product that would result from an alternative design; (6) the adverse consequences to the consumer that would result from an alternative design.

Arguments Supporting Adoption of the New Rule

Definition A

The *Cronin* opinion said that its holding that a product must meet ordinary consumer expectations applied to both design defects and manufacturing defects.

The "consumer expectations" standard for design defect is established by "our cases."

The "warranty heritage" of the rule of strict product liability and a prior case (*Greenman*) indicate that one of the purposes of strict product liability is to make sure that a product is fit for its intended use.

Definition B

The expectations of the ordinary consumer cannot be viewed as an exclusive yardstick for design defect because consumers may not know how safe a product could be made. Therefore, if a product's design embodies "excessive preventable danger," it should be considered defective.

It gives a manufacturer an opportunity to avoid liability by demonstrating design trade-offs involved when selecting among design alternatives; manufacturers are not insurers.

It is consistent with the principle that a product rather than a manufacturer's conduct should be the focus of a trier of fact's inquiry. This might not be the focus if the unreasonably dangerous standard were adopted.

Numerous cases, with "varying linguistic formulations," have recognized a similar rule.

One purpose of strict product liability was to relieve the plaintiff of the onerous burden of proof in a negligence cause of action. This rule does that.

Usually defendants have access to most of the information relevant to the factors to be considered under the risk/benefit prong of the definition of design defect. Because defendants generally have the relevant information, and one purpose of strict product liability was to relieve the plaintiff of the onerous burden of proof in a negligence cause of action, it seems appropriate to shift the burden of proof under this test.

Other cases involving design defects have indicated that these are the relevant factors.

Argument Supporting Both Definitions A and B

Other jurisdictions have adopted a similar two-pronged approach.

Legal Rule Alternatives Considered and Rejected

The "Leave Design Defect Undefined" Alternative

Argument Against This Alternative

The Court indicates that "design defect" is a very broad term, applying to a wide range of circumstances, with no precise, generally accepted definition. If design defect were left undefined, some triers of fact might go to the "extreme" of granting recovery whenever the defect caused an injury, while other juries might go to the other "extreme" and "conclude that because the product matches the intended design" no recovery is possible. These two extreme outcomes would violate the generally accepted legal principle that like cases should be treated alike.

Facts of the Case

Plaintiff Barker sustained serious injuries while operating a high-lift loader, manufactured by the defendant, at a construction site. The loader is designed to lift loads of up to 5,000 pounds to a maximum height of 32 feet. The loader is also designed so that the load can be kept level with a lever located near the steering column. The loader was not equipped with seat belts or a roll bar. A wire and pipe cage over the driver's seat afforded the driver some protection from falling objects. The cab of the loader was located at least nine feet behind the lifting forks.

Plaintiff had received only limited instruction on the operation of the loader. The accident occurred while plaintiff was attempting to lift a load of lumber 18 to 20 feet and to place the load on the second story of a building under construction. The terrain on which the loader rested sloped sharply in several directions. During the lift, coworkers noticed that the load was beginning to tip; they shouted to plaintiff to jump from the loader. Plaintiff then leaped from the loader, but while scrambling away he was struck by a piece of falling lumber.

At the conclusion of trial, the jury was instructed "that strict liability for a defect in design of a product is based on a finding that the product was unreasonably dangerous for its intended use . . . ." Jury found for the defendant. Plaintiff appealed on the grounds that the jury instruction was erroneous. On appeal, court found for plaintiff and ordered a retrial.

IV. CONCLUSION

If you would like additional illustrative examples of case briefs for rule creation opinions you might be assigned to read in your first year, visit *www.aspenlawschool.com/books/moorebinder.*

chapter 12

Rule Creation Opinions in the Classroom

Using the *Barker* opinion as an illustrative example, this chapter discusses some of the principal topics commonly addressed in first-year classrooms when discussing and analyzing rule creation opinions.

I. THE NEW LEGAL RULE(S)

A professor will frequently focus the class's attention on the new legal rule created in a court's opinion.

1. Q: Ms. Gonzales, what was the issue in the **trial court** in *Barker*?

2. A: Whether the high-lift loader used by Barker was defective.

3. Q: And what did the jury decide?

4. A: That it was defective.

5. Q: And **on appeal**, what was the issue in *Barker*?

6. A: Whether the definition of design defect given to the jury was correct.

7. Q: And how does the court in *Barker* resolve this issue?

8. A: The court says that the jury was given the wrong definition.

9. Q: And does the court's holding in *Barker* say what definition of design defect the jury should be given?

10. A: The court says that the jury should have been instructed that a product can be defective if it fails to perform as safely as an ordinary consumer would expect, or if the benefits of the design outweigh its risks.

11. Q: Well, that's a fairly good summary of what the court said, but let's be a bit more specific. Mr. Blount, could you tell us exactly

what the court said about consumer expectations and design defect?

12. A: The court says that the jury should have been instructed that a product can be defective if it is being used as it was intended to be used and it fails to perform as safely as an ordinary consumer would expect it to.

13. Q: Did the court say it had to be an intended use of the product?

14. A: It said it had to be either an intended use of the product or a reasonably foreseeable use.

15. Q: And under this consumer expectations prong of design defect, which party has the burden of proof?

16. A: I'm not sure. I think under the consumer expectations test the plaintiff has the burden of proof, but under the design part of the test the burden shifts to the defendant.

17. Q: Well, let's talk about that. . . .

In this example, the professor asks the students to set out the specifics of the new rule announced by the court in *Barker*. As No. 11 illustrates, shorthand statements of the new rule (No. 10) are typically insufficient, and the professor will routinely ask additional questions to flesh out the specifics of a new rule (Nos. 13, 15, and 17).

II. BRINGING OUT AND CRITIQUING THE COURT'S ARGUMENTS

A professor will frequently ask the class to articulate and critique the arguments relied on by a court for creating a new legal rule. These questions will give you and your classmates a chance to practice these two essential skills.

1. Q: Let's talk a bit more about the consumer expectation test. Ms. Franklin, why does the court think we should have that test?

2. A: The court says that its prior cases have established that a product can be defective if it doesn't meet consumer expectations.

3. Q: Does the court say anything about why these prior cases have established that test?

4. A: I think that the court is saying that those prior cases established that the purpose behind products liability is to make sure products are fit for their intended use.

5. Q: But why does the court think that the measuring stick for intended use should be consumer expectations?

6. A: I don't know.

7. Q: Mr. Park, can you help us understand the court's justifications for using consumer expectations as a measuring stick for design defect?

8. A: I think the court is saying that the manufacturer has a pretty good idea about how consumers are likely to use the product, and they ought to make the products safe for that use.

9. Q: Any other reasons, Mr. Park?

10. A: In addition, the court says that . . . [remainder of answer omitted]

11. Q: Mr. Park, you've done an excellent job of setting out for us the arguments in favor of the consumer expectations test announced in *Barker*.

    Now, Mr. Park, I want you to assume that you represent a defendant manufacturer in a strict liability case involving an allegedly defective product in the fictional State of Despair. Your client won at the trial level and the plaintiff has appealed. On appeal, the plaintiff argues that the trial court should have instructed the jury to follow the consumer expectations test for design defect announced in *Barker*, and the case should therefore be sent back to the jury for a new trial.

    You believe that your client will certainly lose the retrial if the jury is instructed to follow the *Barker* consumer expectations test. What arguments might you make to the appellate court in the State of Despair to convince it to reject the *Barker* test?

12. A: I would say that the ordinary consumer expectation is just too vague, so the manufacturer doesn't really know what to do to meet the test. I'd also argue that the ordinary consumer doesn't usually have any idea how safe a product can be made. So, their expectations shouldn't be the standard.

13. Q: Let's look more closely at these arguments made by Mr. Park. Ms. Zolar, assume you represent the plaintiff in this case. How would you respond to Mr. Park's arguments? Let's take the "its just too vague" argument first.

14. A: First of all, I would say that it is no more vague than many of the other analogous standards we have encountered in torts cases. For instance . . .

In this example, the initial portion of the dialogue (Nos. 1–10) makes the *Barker* court's arguments for the consumer expectations test more explicit. As discussed in Chapter 6, learning to state an argument explicitly will help to make sure that judges and opposing parties fully understand the persuasive power of your argument. When discussing rule creation opinions, professors will routinely provide you with opportunities to learn this essential skill.

The second part of the dialogue (Nos. 11–14) begins a critique of a portion of the rule adopted in *Barker*. This sort of critique helps you to appreciate that the legal rules created by rule creation opinions are almost always subject to "sound arguments both ways;" that is, there are virtually always sound arguments that a court should **not** have created the legal rule announced in its opinion. Court opinions often obscure this "both ways" phenomenon by omitting or downplaying arguments that might undermine the rule created by the court.[1]

These critiques will also help you learn to overcome cognitive dissonance. When you read a court's arguments, it may appear that the rule created by the court is the only one that "makes sense." If so, cognitive dissonance may make it difficult for you to later recognize or fairly evaluate counterarguments. These classroom critiques help you to overcome or mitigate the effects of cognitive dissonance and develop a "there must be counterarguments" habit of mind.

Because you benefit from learning to critique the legal rules created by a court, a professor will sometimes engage in a vigorous critique of a legal rule, even though the professor thinks the court created the "right" legal rule.

III. EXPLORING ALTERNATIVE LEGAL RULES

In addition to critiquing the legal rule created in an opinion, a professor may explore alternative legal rules that the court might have adopted, whether or not these alternatives were mentioned in the court's opinion.

1. Q: Ms. Price, you were an economics major as an undergraduate, correct?

2. A: Yes.

3. Q: Are you familiar with the phrase, "least cost avoider"?

4. A: Yes. As I recall, it means the entity that can avoid the costs of an accident most cheaply.

---

1. Such arguments are, however, typically made in the brief by the losing party and sometimes made in a dissenting opinion.

5. Q: What definition of design defect would you suggest a court adopt if a court wanted to impose liability on the least cost avoider?

6. A: I think a court could create a rule that [remainder of answer omitted] . . .

7. Q: Let's assume that the court in *Barker* adopted the least cost avoider rule that you suggest, Ms. Price. Even rules consistent with economic principles must have some adverse consequences associated with them. So, what do you see as the best arguments against the rule you just proposed?

8. A: I'm sorry, but I think the least cost avoider rule I proposed would produce the most efficient result, so I don't see how there can be any arguments against it.

9. Q: Perhaps someone else can help us. Does anyone see any arguments against the rule proposed by Ms. Price? Yes, Mr. Strong?

10. A: I can see several negative consequences to adopting such a rule. It would definitely . . .

Professors will frequently explore alternatives to the legal rule created in a court opinion. Sometimes these alternatives will be suggested by the theories or principles of other disciplines (e.g., economics, moral philosophy, quantitative methods, etc.). This exploration of alternative legal rules should help you to appreciate that a court is simply choosing from multiple alternatives whenever it creates a new legal rule. These sorts of dialogues may also illustrate that your thinking (and a judge's thinking) about what legal rules should be adopted, and the arguments for and against a proposed legal rule, can be informed by a variety of non-legal disciplines.

IV. THE SCOPE OF THE HOLDING

As explained in the introduction to Part Two, the holding in a rule creation opinion is typically **not limited to the facts of the case before the court.** The holdings in rule creation opinions thus typically have broader application than the holdings in rule application opinions. Class dialogues may occasionally explore this subject.

1. Q: Mr. Lee, the *Barker* case involved a high-lift loader. Is the holding in *Barker* limited to cases involving high-lift loaders?

2. A: I don't think so. I think it applies to all products liability cases. At least all such cases in the State of California.

3. Q: Why do you say that?

4. A: The court didn't say that its holding was limited in any way, so I assume it applies to all cases in this area.

5. Q: In several cases we have read earlier in the course, we have talked about the holding being limited to the facts of the case before the court. But in those cases, the court never explicitly said, "our holding in this case is limited to the facts of this case." So why do you think the holding in *Barker* is **not** limited to the facts of that case?

6. A: The facts of the case didn't seem to have that much to do with the court's decision to create the rule that it did. The court was focused on whether the trial court's jury instruction regarding the law of design defect was correct. To answer that question, I think the court had to decide what the legal rule should be for design defects in products liability cases in general. The court did not indicate that it was adopting a design defect rule just for high-lift loaders.

7. Q: So how is the *Barker* opinion different from the opinions in which the court's holding was limited to the facts of the case?

8. A: I'm not sure, but in some of the other cases we have discussed in this course, the appellate court seemed to think that the legal rule the trial court applied to the facts of the case was correct, but that the result reached by the trial court when applying the rule was incorrect. In *Barker* the California Supreme Court concluded that trial court's instruction to the jury was based on an incorrect rule defining design defect.

9. Q: Let's keep in mind Mr. Lee's distinction between cases that apply an incorrect legal rule and cases that apply the correct legal rule, but reach the incorrect result. We'll see if that distinction holds up as we proceed through the course. Now let's assume for the moment that the *Barker* court's opinion does apply to all design defects in products liability cases in California. Let's talk about why the court in *Barker* gets to make a rule of general application to products liability cases. . . .

As this dialogue continues, it might flesh out when and why courts are allowed to create legal rules of broad applicability.

V. HYPOTHETICALS — CREATING ISSUES IN THE NEW RULE

A professor may also provide the class with a hypothetical in which the facts create issues with respect to the application of the new legal rule.

Subsequent class discussions will then develop arguments that might be made to resolve these issues.

1. Q: Ms. Wells, let's see how the rule announced by the court in *Barker* might apply in practice. I want you to assume the following: Ms. Treemont, a long time California resident, buys an 8-foot aluminum ladder and puts it in her garage. Two days later, as she is taking it out of the garage to trim a tree in her backyard, the ladder brushes against an exposed electrical wire just below the ceiling of the garage. Ms. Treemont receives an electrical shock and is seriously injured. She then sues the manufacturer of the ladder, alleging that it was defectively designed under one or both of the *Barker* definitions of design defect. You represent the plaintiff. Let's focus our attention first on the consumer expectations test. What issues, if any, do you see that might arise in this case under this test?

2. A: There might be a problem proving the ladder failed to satisfy the expectations of an ordinary consumer.

3. Q: Why do you say that?

4. A: Well, the purpose of the product liability rule is . . .

In this example, the facts come from the professor's hypothetical. In some instances, a professor may ask you to apply the new rule to the facts in the opinion that created the rule. For example, a professor might ask you to apply the rule announced in *Barker* to the facts in that case. In either event, this sort of exercise allows you to practice the essential skills of proceeding category by category though a legal rule, spotting issues, and constructing arguments to resolve the issues.

VI. THE RELATIONSHIP BETWEEN THE NEW LEGAL RULE AND OTHER LEGAL RULES

A professor may devote some class time to illustrating how the new rule relates to other rules covered in the course.

1. Q: Let's assume that our arguments will persuade a trier of fact that the ladder had a design defective under the consumer expectations test announced in *Barker*. Mr. Axe, is it now clear that Ms. Treemont will prevail at trial in her case against the ladder manufacturer?

2. A: If we have satisfied *Barker's* consumer expectations test, then I think we have conclusively shown that the ladder was defective.

3. Q: I agree. But does satisfying the consumer expectations test establish all the elements our plaintiff has to prove to recover in a products liability action?

4. A: I don't think so. According to the case we read last week, our plaintiff would have to prove that the ladder was a product, that it was defective, and that the defect was the proximate cause of her injuries. If we satisfy the consumer expectations test, we have established only that the ladder was defective. So, we'd also have to prove that the ladder was a product and that there was proximate cause. I think the ladder is definitely a product, so I don't see any problem there, but I'm not sure about the proximate cause issue.

5. Q: We'll talk about whether those are the only elements of a claim for products liability in a few minutes. Right now, let's focus on proximate cause. And just to give our minds a little exercise, let's turn things around and assume we represent the defendant manufacturer. Ms. Moeller, can you make an argument that the ladder, even if it is defective, was not the proximate cause of the plaintiff's injuries?

6. A: I think we can argue that Ms. Treemont's own negligence was the cause of her injuries; she shouldn't have put the ladder so close to exposed wires. And, I think that is relevant to the issue of proximate cause, because under the rule announced in the case of . . .

This dialogue illustrates the relationship between the new rule created in *Barker* and other legal rules governing product liability claims.

VII. THE DYNAMICS AND VARYING CONTENT OF CLASSROOM DISCUSSIONS

This chapter has described several subjects that might be addressed in a classroom discussion of a rule creation opinion. For the sake of clarity and ease of illustration, we have explored each of these subjects separately. An actual classroom discussion, however, will rarely include all of these subjects, nor will the subjects necessarily be addressed in the order in which we have taken them up in this chapter. Thus, when discussing one rule creation opinion, a professor might omit any discussion of the new legal rule or the arguments relied on by the court and proceed directly to a critique of the new rule. In another class discussing such an opinion, the professor may omit any critique and focus exclusively on the arguments relied on by the court to support its decision.

In addition, classroom discussions will not necessarily complete one subject and then move on to another. For example, a professor may begin a dialogue focused on setting out the court's arguments in support of its decision and, without completely exploring that subject, shift the dialogue to a critique of one of the court's arguments, and then return to setting out the arguments made by the court.

Finally, the subjects addressed in the classroom will vary from class to class and professor to professor. Some professors may focus the class's attention on the arguments advanced by the court to support the creation of the new rule, whereas other professors will ignore this topic and concentrate on hypotheticals requiring the class to apply the new rule.

VIII. WHY PROFESSORS ASK QUESTIONS

Professors typically use a questioning format to analyze rule creation opinions for the same reasons they do so when analyzing rule application opinions. The question-and-answer format puts you in the role of a lawyer and provides you with practice and feedback on your analytical skills.

IX. TAKING NOTES

Once again, there is no single note-taking strategy that works for all students. Some students take close to verbatim notes of what goes on in the classroom, and others record relatively little in their class notes. For classes discussing rule creation opinions we suggest that, at a minimum, your class notes include the following.

You should record new information about the topics in your case brief. Thus, for example, if class discussions clarified your understanding of the legal rules created by the court or the arguments advanced in the opinion, your notes should reflect this clarification.

You will also want to record the facts of any hypotheticals the professor provided to the class. Working through the hypotheticals a professor provided during the course is one effective technique for preparing for an exam.

chapter 13

Rule Application and Rule Creation in a Single Opinion

The *Bridges* opinion in Chapter 5 and the *Barker* opinion in Chapter 11 provided you with prototypical examples of two different types of court opinions. The *Bridges* opinion illustrates application of an existing rule to a set of facts. The *Barker* opinion, on the other hand, created a new, broadly applicable legal rule defining the category "design defect," but the opinion did not apply that rule to a set of facts. Many of the opinions you read for class will be like *Bridges* or *Barker*: they will involve prototypical examples of <u>either</u> application of an existing rule <u>or</u> the creation or adoption of one or more new legal rules.

Some of the opinions you read for class will differ from *Bridges* or *Barker* in one or more of the following respects:

(1) In some opinions, it will be unclear whether the court is applying an existing rule or creating a broadly applicable new legal rule.

(2) In some opinions, a court will <u>both</u> create one or more new legal rules and then apply that newly created rule to the facts of the case before the court.

The opinion in *Grutter v. Bollinger* set out below illustrates each of these phenomena.

I. *GRUTTER V. BOLLINGER*, 539 U.S. 306 SUPREME COURT OF THE UNITED STATES (2003)

A. Background Information

Barbara Grutter, a white Michigan resident, applied to the University of Michigan Law School but was not accepted. She then sued the Law School, alleging that its race-conscious admissions program gave some weight to the race of applicants and therefore violated her rights under the Equal Protection Clause of the U.S. Constitution.

There were two main issues addressed in the Court's opinion. First, the Court had to decide whether the goal of student body diversity that the Law School sought to achieve with a race-conscious admissions program constituted a "**compelling state interest.**" The Court answered this question in the affirmative. As you will see, when resolving this issue, it is unclear whether the Court created a broadly applicable new legal rule or applied an existing rule.

Second, the Court had to decide whether the Law School's admissions program was "**narrowly tailored**" to further a compelling state interest. To answer this question, the Court first created a new rule defining "narrowly tailored" in the context of graduate school admissions. Under this new rule, to be "narrowly tailored" an admissions program has to meet the following requirements:

1. It cannot operate as a quota.

2. It must remain flexible enough to ensure that each applicant is evaluated as an individual and not in a way that makes an applicant's race or ethnicity the defining feature of his or her application.

3. It must give serious, good-faith consideration of workable race-neutral alternatives.

4. It must not unduly burden individuals who are not members of the favored racial and ethnic groups.

Finally, the Court applied this new rule to the Law School's admissions program. When applying this new rule, the Court had to decide if the admissions program satisfied each of the four requirements in the new rule the Court created. The Court decided that the program did satisfy each of these four categories; therefore, the Court found that the program was "narrowly tailored."

Because the Court found that the University of Michigan Law School's goal of student body diversity was a "compelling state interest" and the Law School's admissions program to achieve that goal was "narrowly tailored," the Court found that the Law School's admissions program was lawful.

In the version of the Court's opinion set out below, we have **omitted the Court's arguments** and have set out only an edited version of the facts and the Court's decision on the "compelling state interest" and "narrowly tailored" issues.

B. The Court's Opinion in *Grutter v. Bollinger*

Justice O'CONNOR delivered the opinion of the Court.

This case requires us to decide whether the use of race as a factor in student admissions by the University of Michigan Law School (Law School) is unlawful. . . .

[Facts of the Case]

The Law School ranks among the Nation's top law schools. It receives more than 3,500 applications each year for a class of around 350 students. Seeking to "admit a group of students who individually and collectively are among the most capable," the Law School looks for individuals with "substantial promise for success in law school" and "a strong likelihood of succeeding in the practice of law and contributing in diverse ways to the well-being of others." More broadly, the Law School seeks "a mix of students with varying backgrounds and experiences who will respect and learn from each other." In 1992, the dean of the Law School charged a faculty committee with crafting a written admissions policy to implement these goals. In particular, the Law School sought to ensure that its efforts to achieve student body diversity complied with this Court's most recent ruling on the use of race in university admissions. . . . Upon the unanimous adoption of the committee's report by the Law School faculty, it became the Law School's official admissions policy.

The hallmark of that policy is its focus on academic ability coupled with a flexible assessment of applicants' talents, experiences, and potential "to contribute to the learning of those around them." The policy requires admissions officials to evaluate each applicant based on all the information available in the file, including a personal statement, letters of recommendation, and an essay describing the ways in which the applicant will contribute to the life and diversity of the Law School. . . . In reviewing an applicant's file, admissions officials must consider the applicant's undergraduate grade point average (GPA) and Law School Admissions Test (LSAT) score because they are important (if imperfect) predictors of academic success in law school. . . . The policy stresses that "no applicant should be admitted unless we expect that applicant to do well enough to graduate with no serious academic problems." . . .

The policy makes clear, however, that even the highest possible score does not guarantee admission to the Law School. . . . Nor does a low score automatically disqualify an applicant. . . . Rather, the policy requires admissions officials to look beyond grades and test scores to other criteria that are important to the Law School's educational objectives. . . . So-called " 'soft' variables" such as "the enthusiasm of recommenders, the quality of the undergraduate institution, the quality of the applicant's essay, and the areas and difficulty of undergraduate course selection" are all brought to bear in assessing an "applicant's likely contributions to the intellectual and social life of the institution." . . .

The policy aspires to "achieve that diversity which has the potential to enrich everyone's education and thus make a law school class stronger than the sum of its parts." . . . The policy does not restrict the types of diversity contributions eligible for "substantial weight" in the admissions process, but instead recognizes "many possible bases for diversity admissions." . . . The policy does, however, reaffirm the Law School's longstanding commitment to "one particular type of diversity," that is, "racial and ethnic diversity with special reference to the inclusion of students from groups which have been historically discriminated against, like African-Americans, Hispanics and Native Americans, who without this commitment might not be represented in our student body in meaningful numbers." By enrolling a "'critical mass' of [underrepresented] minority students," the Law School seeks to "ensure their ability to make unique contributions to the character of the Law School." . . .

Petitioner Barbara Grutter is a white Michigan resident who applied to the Law School in 1996 with a 3.8 grade point average and 161 LSAT score. The Law School initially placed petitioner on a waiting list, but subsequently rejected her application. In December 1997, petitioner filed suit in the United States District Court for the Eastern District of Michigan against the Law School . . . [alleging] that [the Law School] discriminated against her on the basis of race in violation of the *Fourteenth Amendment* [and] Title VI of the Civil Rights Act of 1964. . . .

Petitioner further alleged that her application was rejected because the Law School uses race as a "predominant" factor, giving applicants who belong to certain minority groups "a significantly greater chance of admission than students with similar credentials from disfavored racial groups." . . . Petitioner also alleged that respondents "had no compelling interest to justify their use of race in the admissions process." . . .

[The First Issue Resolved by the Court— Is Michigan Law School's Interest in Student Body Diversity a "Compelling State Interest"?]

We have held that all racial classifications imposed by government . . . are constitutional only if they are **narrowly tailored** to further **compelling governmental interests** [emphasis added]. . . .

[W]e turn to the question whether the Law School's use of race is justified by a compelling state interest. Before this Court . . . [the Law School asserts] . . . only one justification for their use of race in the admissions process: obtaining "the educational benefits that flow from a diverse student body." . . . In other words, the Law School asks us to recognize, in the context of higher education, a compelling state interest in student body diversity. . . . Today, we hold that the Law School has a compelling interest in attaining a diverse student body. . . .

[The Second Issue Resolved by the Court— Is Michigan's Admissions Program "Narrowly Tailored" To Achieve Student Body Diversity?]

Even in the limited circumstance when drawing racial distinctions is permissible to further a compelling state interest, government is still "constrained in how it may pursue that end: [T]he means chosen to accomplish the [government's] asserted purpose must be specifically and narrowly framed to accomplish that purpose. . . ."

. . .

We find that the Law School's admissions program bears the hallmarks of a narrowly tailored plan . . .

[First requirement for "narrowly tailored" — the program does not operate as a quota]

We are satisfied that the Law School's admissions program . . . does not operate as a **quota**. . . . [emphasis added]

. . .

[Second requirement for "narrowly tailored" — evaluation as an individual]

That a race-conscious admissions program does not operate as a quota does not, by itself, satisfy the requirement of individualized consideration. When using race as a "plus" factor in university admissions, a university's admissions program must remain flexible enough to ensure that **each applicant is evaluated as an individual and not in a way that makes an applicant's race or ethnicity the defining feature of his or her application** [emphasis added]. . . .

Here, the Law School engages in a highly individualized, holistic review of each applicant's file, giving serious consideration to all the ways an applicant might contribute to a diverse educational environment. The Law School affords this individualized consideration to applicants of all races.

. . .

[Third requirement for "narrowly tailored" — consideration of race neutral alternatives]

Petitioner and the United States argue that the Law School's plan is not narrowly tailored because race-neutral means exist to obtain the educational benefits of student body diversity that the Law School seeks. We disagree. Narrow tailoring does not require exhaustion of every conceivable race-neutral alternative. Nor does it require a university to choose between maintaining a reputation for excellence or fulfilling a commitment to provide educational opportunities to members of all racial groups. . . . Narrow tailoring does, however, require **serious, good faith consideration of workable race-neutral alternatives that will achieve the diversity the university seeks.** [emphasis added]

We agree with the Court of Appeals that the Law School sufficiently considered workable race-neutral alternatives.

. . .

[Fourth requirement for "narrowly tailored" — absence of undue burden on those not members of favored groups]

We acknowledge that "there are serious problems of justice connected with the idea of preference itself.". . . Narrow tailoring, therefore, requires that a race-conscious admissions program not unduly harm members of any racial group. . . . To be narrowly tailored, a race-conscious admissions program must "**not unduly burden individuals who are not members of the favored racial and ethnic groups.**" [emphasis added] . . . We are satisfied that the Law School's admissions program does not.

. . .

In summary, the *Equal Protection Clause* does not prohibit the Law School's narrowly tailored use of race in admissions decisions to further a compelling interest in obtaining the educational benefits that flow from a diverse student body. . . .

II. ANALYSIS OF THE RULES APPLIED AND CREATED IN *GRUTTER V. BOLLINGER*

A. Student Body Diversity in Higher Education as a "Compelling State Interest" — Does the Court Apply an Existing Rule or Create a Broadly Applicable New Legal Rule?

The first question addressed by the Court is whether diversity in higher education constitutes a "compelling state interest." One might see this as a rule application issue. That is, the Court is deciding whether the University of Michigan Law School's pursuit of diversity in its student body satisfies the existing legal category "compelling state interest;" and the Court holds that the Law School's pursuit of this goal does satisfy this category.

On the other hand, one might see the Court's holding as creating a broadly applicable new legal rule defining the existing legal category "compelling state interest." Under this interpretation, the Court created the following new broadly applicable legal rule: The pursuit of student body diversity in admissions in higher education constitutes a "compelling state interest." If one sees the Court as creating this new legal rule, then the Law School's interest in a diverse student body is clearly a "compelling state interest."

1. Why It Matters Whether the Court Is Creating a New Legal Rule Defining "Compelling State Interest" in Higher Education

Recall that when a court applies an existing rule to a set of facts, its holding is usually "limited to the facts of the case" before the court.

If the Court in *Grutter* is simply saying that the **University of Michigan Law School's** pursuit of diversity in its student body satisfies the category "compelling state interest," the Court's holding is arguably limited to the facts of the Michigan case.

Recall, however, that a holding creating a new legal rule is typically not limited to the facts of the case in which the rule was created. If the Court's holding resolving the "compelling state interest" issue is seen as creating a new rule defining student body diversity in higher education as a compelling state interest, it will arguably apply to all future cases involving race conscious admissions programs in higher education.

The question of whether the court is applying an existing rule or creating a new legal rule of broad applicability can be critically important for you in law practice. Assume, for example, that you represent a state law school in Florida with a race-conscious admissions program allegedly designed to produce student body diversity. The school is being sued by a white student who was denied admission and claims that the school's admissions program violates the Equal Protection Clause of the U.S. Constitution.

If the *Grutter* holding created a rule that student body diversity in higher education is a compelling state interest, then the Florida state law school's pursuit of diversity would obviously be a compelling state interest.

If *Grutter* held only that the **Michigan Law School's** pursuit of diversity constituted a "compelling state interest," however, you would have to argue that the facts of the Florida law school's case satisfy the "compelling state interest" category. One of many arguments you might make on that issue on behalf of the Florida school would be an argument by analogy to the *Grutter* case.

2. Classroom Dialogues About Whether *Grutter v. Bollinger* Applied an Existing Rule or Created a Broadly Applicable New Legal Rule

As the example below illustrates, a classroom dialogue may address the question of whether a court's holding applies an existing rule or creates a broadly applicable new legal rule.

1. Q: Mr. Mushovic, I would like us to address the question of the scope of the Court's holding on the "compelling state interest" issue in *Grutter.* Let's consider how broad or narrow the Court's holding was. I want you to assume that the University of Maine Law School has established a race-conscious admissions program for the purpose of obtaining student body diversity. Mr. Simpson, a white applicant who was denied admission to the Law School, has filed suit alleging that the admissions program violates his rights under the Equal Protection Clause of the U.S. Constitution. Does

the holding in *Grutter* establish that the Maine Law School's interest in student body diversity is a "compelling" state interest?

2. A: Yes. I think *Grutter* held that trying to create student body diversity at a state law school was a compelling state interest.

3. Q: Does anyone disagree with Mr. Mushovic? Yes, Ms. Oshima?

4. A: I think the *Grutter* holding was narrower than that. I think the Court just held that under the facts in that case the University of Michigan Law School had a compelling state interest in student body diversity; the Court didn't hold that student body diversity in a state law school was always a compelling state interest.

5. Q: Mr. Mushovic, it looks like you're going to have to defend your position. What arguments can you make that the Court's holding in *Grutter* established that student body diversity at a state law school was, as a matter of law, a compelling state interest?

6. A: The Court says that they have been asked to recognize student body diversity as a compelling state interest "in the context of higher education." The Court could have said, but did *not* say, that they had been asked to recognize it as a compelling state interest "in the context of the circumstances presented by the case of the Michigan Law School." So I guess my first argument is that the Court's language seems to characterize this issue in broad terms that would make their decision generally applicable to programs of higher education. So I think we can infer from the Court's language that it did intend to create a legal rule that an effort to create diversity in a student body at an institution of higher education is a compelling state interest.

7. Q: Ms. Oshima, do you wish to respond?

8. A: I agree that we have to look closely at the language the Court uses in its opinion. The language I would focus on is, "we hold that the *Law School* has a compelling interest in attaining a diverse student body." The Court could have said, but did *not* say, "we hold that student body diversity in higher education is a compelling state interest and therefore Michigan has a compelling state interest in this case." So I guess my first argument is that we can infer that the Court's language describing its *holding* on this issue seems to limit its holding to the facts of this case.[1] In addition . . .

---

1. You will note that in this dialogue that both students rely on language in the Court's opinion for arguments pointing in opposite directions. Court opinions often contain language that can support both an argument for a broad holding and an argument for a narrow holding.

In law practice, you may have to make arguments about whether a previous court's holding is narrow and limited to the "facts of the case" in which it was announced, or else creates a broad new legal rule that is applicable beyond the facts of the case in which the rule was created. As this brief example illustrates, a professor may structure classroom dialogues to allow you and your colleagues to practice and receive feedback on this important skill.

B. Is Michigan's Program "Narrowly Tailored"? — Announcing a New Legal Rule and Then Applying the New Rule

The second issue addressed by the Court is whether the University of Michigan Law School's admissions program is "narrowly tailored." The Court resolves this issue by announcing a new legal rule that defines "narrowly tailored" in the context of admissions programs in higher education.[2] The new legal rule might be stated as follows:

To be "**narrowly tailored**" an admissions plan must:

1. Not operate as a quota.

2. Remain flexible enough to ensure that each applicant is evaluated as an individual and not in a way that makes an applicant's race or ethnicity the defining feature of his or her application.

3. Require serious, good-faith consideration of workable race-neutral alternatives that will achieve the diversity the university seeks.

4. Not unduly burden individuals who are not members of the favored racial and ethnic groups.

These criteria defining "narrowly tailored" seem to create a legal rule that applies to the University of Michigan Law School's admissions program, and will also apply to future cases involving other admissions programs in higher education.

The Court's new rule will provide guidance to other colleges and universities seeking to comply with the "narrowly tailored" constitutional requirement of equal protection law. The new rule will also provide guidance to lower federal courts to assure that the same legal standard will be applied to all similar admissions programs in the future. Thus, this new rule increases the probability that similar cases in this area will have similar outcomes.

---

2. In *Grutter*, the Court relies to some extent on previous cases to support its new rule defining "narrowly tailored" in the context of graduate school admissions programs. So it is perhaps unclear to what extent the Court is creating a totally new definition of "narrowly tailored" or adopting portions of a definition announced in prior cases. It appears likely, however, that the Court is announcing a legal rule defining the category "narrowly tailored" in the context of admissions programs at institutions of higher education.

In addition to announcing a rule defining "narrowly tailored" in the context of admissions in higher education, the Court also proceeds category by category through the new rule and decides if the Michigan Law School's admissions program satisfies each category. In other words, the Court decides that the facts of the case satisfy each of the following categories: (1) does not operate as a quota; (2) remains flexible enough to ensure that each applicant is evaluated as an individual, and not in a way that makes an applicant's race or ethnicity the defining feature of his or her application; (3) provides for serious, good-faith consideration of workable race-neutral alternatives that will achieve the diversity the university seeks; and (4) does not unduly burden individuals who are not members of the favored racial and ethnic groups.[3]

When discussing the *Grutter* opinion in class, a professor might examine the Court's arguments justifying the creation of the new rule defining "narrowly tailored" in the context of admissions programs in higher education. These classroom dialogues would be similar to the dialogues set forth in Chapters 6–9.

In addition, a professor might also examine the Court's arguments that the Michigan program satisfies categories (1)–(4) in the newly created rule defining "narrowly tailored." These classroom dialogues would be similar to the dialogues set forth in Chapter 12.

III. PREPARING FOR CLASS WHEN AN OPINION INVOLVES BOTH RULE APPLICATION AND RULE CREATION

In Chapter 5 we discussed preparing for class when reading rule application opinions. In Chapter 11, we discussed preparing for class when reading rule creation opinions. To prepare for class when a single opinion does both, you can follow the preparation suggestions in Chapters 5 and 11.

---

3. The text assumes (1)–(4) are each composed of a single legal category. Reasonable people might see more than one category in (1)–(4).

Arguments Revisited, Judicial Decision-Making, and Client Counseling

Part Three contains three chapters. Chapter 14 looks more closely at three of the argument types discussed in Parts One and Two, namely, arguments by analogy, principle arguments, and goal arguments. This chapter also discusses narrative arguments and the burden of proof standards attached to legal categories.

Chapter 15 examines the inherently subjective nature of judicial decision-making in rule application and rule creation opinions.

Chapter 16 explains why the argument construction and evaluation skills you learn in your first year will help you counsel clients when you enter law practice.

chapter 14

Arguments Revisited

Chapter 4 provided you with simple, prototypical, illustrative examples of six types of arguments you might use when making arguments to resolve issues of rule application or when arguing for the creation of new legal rules. This chapter examines in more detail three of the six types of arguments: arguments by analogy, principle arguments, and goal arguments. The chapter also examines narrative arguments, a type of argument not discussed in Chapter 4. The chapter concludes with a discussion of legal arguments and the burden of proof.

I. COURT OPINIONS AND ARGUMENTS BY ANALOGY

Court opinions are one of the most common sources for arguments by analogy. In its simplest form, an argument by analogy from a court opinion first explains why the issue decided in the opinion (either an issue of rule application or a decision regarding the creation of a new legal rule) is similar to an issue under consideration; the argument then asserts that the issue under consideration should be decided in the same way that the issue was decided in the court opinion. Establishing that an issue in a court opinion is similar to an issue to be decided can involve **feature** or **attribute** comparison. That is, similarity is established by simply comparing similar features or attributes of the previously decided issue and the issue to be decided.

When similarity is established only by feature or attribute comparison, an argument by analogy may have intuitive appeal and persuasive force. Feature or attribute comparison alone may not produce a persuasive argument by analogy, however, because such a comparison does not explicitly explain **why the similarities justify a similar result**. For example, a skateboard and a bicycle share common attributes; both are non-polluting and can be used for transportation. It may not be obvious, however, why or if those common attributes should matter when deciding if a case holding that a skateboard is not a vehicle justifies a similar result when deciding if a bicycle is a vehicle.

A. Dragging and Dropping Arguments from a Prior Court Opinion

Recall from Chapter 9 that you can sometimes "drag and drop" the arguments from a court opinion. When you use this approach, you drag arguments from a court opinion and drop them on the facts of the new case to be decided. You then explain why the arguments from the court opinion apply under the facts of the new case. You can often use the "drag and drop" approach to increase the persuasive power of an argument by analogy. As the example below illustrates, dragging and dropping arguments from a court opinion will help you to explain why similar features or attributes between the issue in the opinion and the issue in the new case should dictate a similar result.

Assume that you represent Dan Lucas, who was riding his bicycle in a public park in the State of Replication and is charged with violating a statute prohibiting the use of "vehicles" in public parks. In *People v. Morikawa*, the highest appellate court in the State of Replication held that a skateboard was not a "vehicle" under this statute. You make the following argument:

> Your Honor, a bicycle should not be considered a vehicle within the meaning of the statute at issue in this case. In *People v. Morikawa*, the court held that a skateboard was not a "vehicle" under this statute.
>
> In deciding that a skateboard was not a "vehicle" under this statute, the court in *Morikawa* stated that promoting quiet enjoyment of our parks was one of the **goals** behind the statute, and that a finding that a skateboard was not a vehicle was consistent with this goal because a skateboard produced relatively little noise and therefore its use did not interfere with quiet enjoyment of our parks. A bicycle typically makes even less noise than a skateboard, so it, too, will not interfere with the goal of providing quiet enjoyment of our parks.
>
> The *Morikawa* court also stated that a skateboard is sometimes used by individuals for transportation and a finding that it was not a "vehicle" within the meaning of the statute would encourage a non-polluting form of transportation. Bicycles are routinely used for transportation and a finding that a bicycle is not a "vehicle" would similarly encourage the positive **consequence** of encouraging the use of a non-polluting form of transportation.
>
> Finally, the *Morikawa* court also recognized the **principle** that traditional park recreational activities, such as skateboarding, should not be prohibited when they pose only a small risk of injury to

pedestrians. Bike riding is similarly a traditional recreational activity in parks, and it also creates only a small risk of injury to park patrons. Indeed, the risk of injury is potentially smaller with bicycles than skateboards. Bicycles are equipped with brakes and are therefore easier to stop.

The rationales set forth by the court in *Morikawa* apply with equal force to both a skateboard and a bicycle. Therefore, just as a skateboard is not considered a "vehicle" under this statute, so too a bicycle should not be considered a "vehicle."

The court in *Morikawa* relied on three arguments to decide that a skateboard was not a vehicle: a goal argument (promoting quiet enjoyment of parks was one of the purposes behind the statute), a consequences argument (reducing pollution), and a principle argument (traditional park recreational activities should not be prohibited when they entail a relatively small risk of injury). In this example, you go beyond mere feature comparison and drag and drop those three arguments, and explain why they apply to a case involving a bicycle.

B. Responding to an Adversary's Arguments by Analogy — Distinguishing Prior Court Opinions

In law practice and law school, you need to be able to make arguments by analogy and also respond to such arguments when made by an adversary. A common response to an adversary's argument by analogy based on a prior court opinion is to "distinguish" the prior opinion. One way to distinguish a prior opinion involves using some combination of the feature comparison and the dragging and dropping the prior argument approaches discussed above. When you use a feature comparison approach to distinguish a prior opinion, you will focus on **differences** in features or attributes rather than similarities. When you use a drag and drop the prior arguments approach, you explain that the arguments in the prior case do **not** make sense under the facts of the case currently under consideration.

To provide you with practice in the skill of distinguishing court opinions, as the dialogue below illustrates, in class your professors may ask you to distinguish prior court opinions.

1. Q: [By Professor] Ms. Aaron, last week we read the *Grutter* case, in which the Supreme Court upheld the University of Michigan Law School's race-conscious admissions program. I want you to assume that you are an attorney in the State of Harmony. You represent the State, which has a university for chiropractors that has a race-conscious admissions program. As in *Grutter*, the State of Harmony

asserts only one justification for the use of race in the admissions process: obtaining the educational benefits that flow from a diverse student body. Can you use the *Grutter* case to argue that the State of Harmony's interest in obtaining a diverse student body is a "compelling" state interest?

2. A: Definitely. I think *Grutter* is directly analogous to this case. There are several similar features in the two cases, and some of the arguments that the court relied on in *Grutter* make perfect sense in this case. First of all . . . [remainder of answer omitted]

3. Q: Thank you, Ms. Aaron. Now, let's see if we can distinguish the *Grutter* case. Mr. Bergman, I want you to assume that you represent a white applicant to the Harmony Chiropractic University who is challenging the race-conscious admissions program as a violation of the Equal Protection Clause in the U.S. Constitution. You want to argue that the State of Harmony's interest in obtaining a diverse student body is **not** a "compelling" state interest. Ms. Aaron has made some sound arguments that *Grutter* is analogous to this case. Can you **distinguish** the *Grutter* opinion?

4. A: Yes. There are significant differences between the two cases. Lawyers are frequently present in public, both in the courtroom and in the media, and chiropractors are not. I think it's more important to have racial diversity in groups that regularly appear in public. Furthermore, chiropractors account for only a small percentage of the health care profession; lawyers account for an overwhelming proportion of the legal profession.

     In addition, some of the arguments that the Court relied on in *Grutter* don't seem to apply in this case. For instance, the Court found that the University of Michigan Law School's interest in diversity was compelling, at least in part, because it facilitated effective participation by members of all racial and ethnic groups in the civic life of the United States. I don't think that going to chiropractic school will increase someone's ability to participate in civic life. The court also argued that racial diversity was a compelling interest in *Grutter* because law school provides the training ground for a large number of our nation's leaders. Again, I don't think this is true for a chiropractic university. So, I would say that two of the consequences arguments made by the Court in *Grutter* don't apply to the case of a chiropractic school.

5. Q: I think you have identified some of the arguments the Court relied on in *Grutter* that do not seem to apply in this context, but I would like to press you a bit on some of the factual distinctions you made. You say that chiropractors account for only a small percentage of the health care profession and lawyers account for

an overwhelming proportion of the legal profession. Assuming that is true, why should that distinction matter when deciding whether racial diversity in the student body of a chiropractic school is a "compelling" state interest?

6. A: Well, I'm not really sure. When I pointed out that difference it had an intuitive appeal to me, but right now I can't really explain why it should matter.

7. Q: Perhaps one of your classmates can help. Yes, Ms. Kim?

8. A: I think it matters because . . .

In this example, a student (Mr. Bergman) distinguishes *Grutter* by pointing out feature differences in the two cases and explaining why prior arguments do not seem to apply when dragged and dropped from *Grutter* onto the facts of the professor's hypothetical (No. 4). This dialogue also illustrates that a professor (or a judge in practice) may require you to explain why feature differences matter (Nos. 5 and 6).

II. INFERRING PRINCIPLES FROM COURT OPINIONS

As you read and discuss court opinions and listen to classroom lectures and dialogues in law school, you will encounter many expressly stated principles. For example, your Contracts professor may tell you that in contract law it is a generally accepted principle that ambiguities in a contract should ordinarily be interpreted against the party that drafted the contract. Similarly, a court opinion may announce the principle that words in legal rules should generally be given their ordinary meaning. You may be able to use these expressly stated principles to make principle arguments in law school or in practice.

Court opinion(s) can sometimes be used to infer a principle, **even though the principle is not expressly stated in the opinion(s)**. Once you have inferred a principle from court opinion(s), you can then use it to make a principle argument to resolve a rule application issue or to argue for the creation of a new legal rule.

You can sometimes infer a principle from one or more prior court opinions by explaining why the inferred principle is consistent with the results and/or the arguments made in the prior opinion(s). The following hypothetical illustrates the process of inferring a principle from opinions and then using that principle to make a principle argument.

Assume that several court opinions have reversed convictions that were originally obtained primarily on the basis of eyewitness identifications. In each opinion, the reversal was based on post-conviction DNA evidence establishing the defendant's innocence. You now represent a criminal defendant who was convicted at trial. On appeal, you make the following argument:

> Your Honor, we have cited several cases in our brief in which DNA evidence has led to the reversal of convictions. In each of these cases, the original conviction was obtained almost exclusively on the basis of an eyewitness identification. These cases stand for the principle that, standing alone, eyewitness identifications should be viewed with caution. This principle justifies a change in the standard jury instruction for evaluating eyewitness identifications. In cases such as this one, with no evidence establishing the defendant's presence at the scene of the crime other than the testimony of a single eyewitness, the standard jury instruction should be changed to add the following language: "Eyewitness identifications should be closely scrutinized, especially when there is no substantial additional evidence connecting the defendant to the crime." Because this language was not included in the instructions given in the trial court below, the conviction should be overturned and a new trial ordered.

In this example, you use the results of prior cases to infer the principle that, standing alone, eyewitness identifications should be viewed with caution. As this example illustrates, when principles are inferred from court opinion(s), the opinions are usually said to "stand for" the inferred principle. Having inferred the principle, you then use that principle to argue for a change in the legal rule reflected in the standard jury instruction.

You may want to infer a principle when answering a law school exam. Assume that in your criminal law class you read three opinions where convictions were obtained based primarily on eyewitness identifications and then subsequently overturned because of exculpatory DNA evidence. On a criminal law exam, you are given the following proposed new jury instruction: "Eyewitness identifications should be closely scrutinized, especially when there is no substantial additional evidence connecting the defendant to the crime." The exam asks you to make arguments for and against the proposed new instruction. One of your arguments in favor of such an instruction might look like the principle argument set forth above.

In the preceding example, the opinions used to infer a principle all involved criminal convictions based on eyewitness testimony. In some instances, however, especially in law practice, you may be able to infer a principle from opinions in several areas of law. Consider the following hypothetical.

Assume Harry Hiker falls and breaks his leg while hiking in the Rescue Mountains. Sally Callous is hiking in the same mountains and comes across the injured Harry. Harry explains that he has broken his leg and asks Sally for assistance. Sally ignores Harry's request, hikes to the top of the mountain, and camps out. Harry is rescued the next morning but loses two toes as a result of frostbite from the overnight exposure. Harry sues Sally alleging that she had a duty to assist him and that her breach of that duty proximately caused his frostbite and the resulting amputation of his toes. You represent Harry. The trial court dismissed Harry's case, citing the legal rule that people do not have a duty to rescue a stranger. On appeal, you represent Harry and you ask the appellate court to adopt the following new legal rule:

> When people know that a stranger is at risk of significant bodily injury and is unable to adequately protect him/herself, they have a duty to take reasonable steps to aid a stranger.

One principle argument you make in support of your proposed new rule is as follows:

> Your Honor, the rule we ask the court to adopt in this case is consistent with prior decisions of this court. In the cases cited in the plaintiff's brief, landlords have consistently been held to have a duty to take steps to protect tenants from dangers likely to arise from failures to maintain and repair the rented premises. Many tenants in modern buildings cannot find and repair defects in the leased premises themselves. Similarly, plaintiff's brief cites several decisions in which this court has held that landowners have a duty to take steps to protect people on neighboring land from dangers on the owner's land. People on neighboring land typically cannot protect themselves from dangers posed by conditions on another's property. Finally, many decisions referred to in plaintiff's brief have held that sellers of products have a duty to try to protect buyers and potential users of their products from defects in those products. People buying modern-day products may not be able to protect themselves from non-obvious defects arising from the product's design or manufacture. These prior decisions by this court have established the principle that people should have a duty to make reasonable efforts to protect those who they know are in danger of injury and who they know cannot protect themselves. The rule the plaintiff asks you to adopt in this case is consistent with this established principle.

III. INFERRING GOALS

In some instances, the goal(s) behind a rule or set of rules will be well established or undisputed. For example, your professor, a court opinion, or other assigned readings in a course may announce that one of the goals behind the criminal law is deterrence of future misconduct. You may then be able to use a well-established goal to make a goal argument in the classroom or on an exam by explaining how the goal is either consistent or inconsistent with the result for which you are arguing.

In many instances, however, especially in law practice, the goal(s) behind a rule or set of rules will **not** be well established. When this is the case, to make a goal argument, you may first infer a goal and then explain how the result you are arguing for will further or frustrate that inferred goal.

You can sometimes infer a goal from the circumstances surrounding the enactment of a legal rule. The following example illustrates such an inference argument. Assume Mike Miner, a 17-year-old, approaches Paul Byers, a 25-year-old about to enter an establishment selling alcohol. Miner offers to pay Byers $10.00 to purchase 2 six-packs of beer for him. Byers accepts the offer. Immediately after consuming the beer purchased for him by Byers, Miner's car strikes and kills a pedestrian in a crosswalk. The incident receives extensive coverage in the newspapers and on television. Shortly thereafter, the legislature passes a statute making it a felony to "purchase alcohol for a minor."

A few months after the statute is enacted, Steve Derian buys beer for a party at his home. Derian knew that Sal and Sammy, two 17-year-old friends of his son, would attend the party. Sal and Sammy attend the party, consume some of the beer purchased by Derian, and are arrested for driving under the influence of alcohol when driving home from the party. Derian is then arrested and charged with violating the statute prohibiting the purchase of alcohol for a minor. You represent Derian, and you make the following argument:

> Your Honor, the goal behind the statute that Mr. Derian is charged with violating was to prevent people from purchasing alcohol *at the request of* a minor. As described in the defense brief submitted to the court, the statute in this case was passed immediately after the media gave extensive coverage to an incident in which Paul Byers purchased alcohol at the request of a minor who then became intoxicated and killed an innocent pedestrian. The debate on this statute in the legislature referred to the Byers incident as one justification for passage of the statute at issue in this case. We can therefore infer that by passing the statute the legislature intended to prohibit people from purchasing alcohol *at the request of* a minor, as Byers had done. The purpose of this statute is not to prohibit adults from purchasing alcohol for use at a function that may be attended by minors, which is all Mr. Derian did in this case. Therefore, you should find that Mr. Derian did not violate this statute.

Your argument first asks the court to infer the purpose or goal of the statute from circumstances surrounding its enactment. It then explains why a conviction of your client would not be consistent with this inferred goal.

In the above example, the circumstances surrounding the enactment of the statute are used as circumstantial evidence to infer the goal behind the statute. There are, however, other types of evidence you might use to infer a goal behind a rule. You might rely on, for instance, the language used in a rule, the results of cases interpreting a rule, or the well-established goals behind similar rules.

You may want to infer a goal on a law school exam. For example, assume on a civil procedure exam you are given a new statute relating to the information that may be obtained in discovery by parties to a lawsuit. The exam does not indicate the goal or purpose behind this new rule or include any of the circumstances surrounding its adoption. You may want to argue that the goal behind the new statute on the exam can be inferred from well-established goals behind similar statutes you discussed in the course. You might then be able to explain why the inferred goal might be furthered or frustrated by a decision on one of the issues raised on the exam.

IV. NARRATIVE ARGUMENTS

In addition to the six types of arguments discussed in Chapter 4, lawyers and courts routinely rely on a narrative; that is, a version or story of what happened and why it happened, to help persuade an audience. A narrative may have persuasive force because, among other things, it appeals to a decision maker's intuitive sense of justice or fairness or resonates with a decision-maker's prior direct or analogous experience about how events typically unfold. We refer to a narrative with persuasive force as a narrative argument.

Narrative arguments typically do not **expressly** identify a specific legal category, nor do such arguments typically **expressly** appeal to goals, principles, consequences, analogies, precedents, or inferences.

An illustrative example of a narrative argument is set out below.

In biblical times, two women lived together in a house of prostitution, and they both gave birth to a son on the same day. Both mothers slept in adjacent beds with their child at their side. Two months after the births, one mother rolled over in her bed while asleep and accidentally smothered her child. The mother awoke in the night and realized her child was dead. She then put her dead child in the bed of the other mother and took the other mother's living child into her bed. In the morning, both mothers claimed that the live child was theirs and that the other had smothered her child. Both mothers went to King

Solomon to resolve their custody dispute. Solomon listened to both mothers and then called for a sword to split the live baby in two, leaving each mother with half. One mother accepted the verdict, saying, "It shall be neither yours nor mine; cut it in two!" The other mother said, "Please, my lord give her the live child, only don't kill it!" Solomon awarded the child to the mother who was willing to give up custody to save the child's life.

People reading this narrative may tend to be persuaded that Solomon's decision was correct, even though the narrative makes no explicit references to goals, consequences, principles, analogies, or inferences.

The statement of facts in a court's opinion is frequently organized into a narrative argument constructed and designed, at least in part, to persuade the reader of the opinion that the court's decision is correct.[1]

In law practice, you will frequently use narrative arguments. Your statement of facts to a judge, jury, or other decision-maker will routinely be designed, at least in part, to persuade a decision-maker to decide in your client's favor. In your first-year legal writing course, your professor will probably explicitly address the question of how to construct a persuasive narrative or "statement of facts," and you will have an opportunity to practice this skill when you complete some of your writing assignments in that course.

You may intuitively make narrative arguments in your first-year classrooms, especially when a professor asks you if you agree with a court's decision. When you make a narrative argument, however, as illustrated in the example below, a professor will frequently require you to go beyond the narrative and articulate one or more of the arguments described in Chapter 4.

1. Q: [By Professor] Mr. Polanski, today we will look at the *Palsgraf* case. The majority opinion found for the defendant and against Ms. Palsgraf. Do you agree with the majority opinion?

2. A: No. I don't think the majority decision was fair. She was just standing on a railroad station platform minding her own business waiting for a train to take her to the beach. A railroad employee pushes a passenger onto a moving train, causing the passenger to drop a package, which explodes. The explosion knocks over some scales on the end of the platform and the scales hit and injure Ms. Palsgraf. She couldn't do anything to avoid the injury, and she didn't do anything to contribute to her injury. She should be able to recover.

---

1. To illustrate that a court has constructed the statement of facts as a narrative argument, some of your professors may provide you with additional facts beyond the facts stated in an opinion to illustrate how the court has selected and characterized the facts to construct a narrative argument in its statement of facts.

3. Q: But why do the facts that you have stated justify a recovery for Ms. Palsgraf?

4. A: My facts justify a recovery for Ms. Palsgraf because they show that it would be fair or just for her to recover.

5. Q: You have certainly stated the facts in a way that suggests Ms. Palsgraf is an innocent victim, and that suggestion might help to convince a jury or a judge that it is fair to find for Ms. Palsgraf. But let's assume, Mr. Polanski, that, as is often the case, you appear before a judge who is not convinced that Ms. Palsgraf should recover simply because she appears to be an innocent victim. The judge wants you to focus more directly on the legal category at issue in this case. Let's see if we can expand your argument repertoire so you can persuade these sorts of judges.

   The majority in *Palsgraf* says that the railroad doesn't owe a duty to Ms. Palsgraf because she was not within the "zone of danger." Can you make an argument under the facts of this case Ms. Palsgraf **was** within the "zone of danger"?

6. A: I can't think of any.

7. Q: Can you identify any positive consequences that might result from a finding that Ms. Palsgraf was within the zone of danger?

8. A: Well, I think such a finding might . . .

In this dialogue, the student provides a narrative argument that suggests that it would be fair for Ms. Palsgraf to recover because she did nothing to cause or contribute to her injury, and the railroad employee's actions caused the explosion that ultimately injured Ms. Palsgraf (No. 2).

The professor then asks the student why the facts in the narrative justify a recovery for Ms. Palsgraf (No. 3). This sort of question by the professor sometimes creates the mistaken impression that the professor (and by implication, legal education) is not concerned with what is "fair" or "just." As the questions in Nos. 5 and 7 make clear, however, professors may push you beyond narrative arguments so that your argument repertoire will include both narratives and one or more of the six types of arguments discussed in Chapter 4, which may be essential for convincing legally trained decision-makers.

V. RULE APPLICATION AND THE BURDEN OF PROOF

For some legal categories, a burden of proof attaches to the question of whether facts satisfy or fail to satisfy the category. For example, assume that a defendant is on trial for first-degree murder, and that to establish this crime the prosecution must show that the defendant "intended to kill" the victim. The burden of proof attached to the category "intent to kill" in such a case is "beyond a reasonable doubt." Therefore, assuming the defendant does not admit that he intended to kill the victim, the fact-finder at trial (usually a jury) should listen to the arguments from the prosecution and the defense and then decide whether the evidence establishes "intent to kill beyond a reasonable doubt."

On appeal, the burden of proof applied at the trial court level remains attached to the question of whether the facts satisfy or fail to satisfy a legal category. For example, assume in the previous example that the jury finds the defendant guilty of first-degree murder. You represent the defendant and appeal on the grounds that there was insufficient evidence introduced at trial for the jury to find "intent to kill beyond a reasonable doubt." After listening to your arguments and those of the prosecutor, the appellate court will decide whether the evidence at trial was sufficient for a reasonable jury to find that there was "intent to kill beyond a reasonable doubt." If the appellate court decides that there was sufficient evidence for a reasonable jury to conclude that there was "intent to kill beyond a reasonable doubt," it will sustain the jury's finding on this issue. If the appellate court decides that there was insufficient evidence for a reasonable jury to conclude that there was "intent to kill beyond a reasonable doubt," it will overturn the jury's finding on this issue, and also overturn the defendant's conviction for first-degree murder.

When a burden of proof attaches to the question of whether the facts satisfy or fail to satisfy a legal category, that issue is generally said to involve a "question of fact." For some legal categories, no burden of proof is attached to the question of whether the facts satisfy or fail to satisfy the category. For example, assume that a defendant is charged with a criminal misdemeanor for riding his bicycle in the park in violation of the "no vehicles in the park" statute. The defendant moves to dismiss the case on the grounds that a bicycle is not a "vehicle" within the meaning of the statute. After listening to the arguments for both the prosecution and the defense, the trial judge would decide whether or not a bicycle satisfies the legal category "vehicle." When making this decision, the trial judge need not apply any burden of proof. Similarly, if the question of whether a bicycle is a vehicle is raised on appeal, an appellate court need not apply any burden of proof when resolving this issue. When no burden of proof attaches to the question of whether the facts satisfy or fail to satisfy a legal category, that issue is generally referred to as a "question of law."

In many of your first-year courses, your professors may address questions such as: Which legal categories raise questions of law and why? Which legal categories raise questions of fact and why? Do some legal categories raise questions of both fact and law, or mixed questions of fact and law? If there is a burden of proof attached to a legal category, what is the burden and why does that particular burden apply? These questions can be quite complicated, and we will not address them here. However, understanding that a burden of proof can attach to some legal categories may help you to understand some of the appellate court opinions you read, especially those opinions addressing the issue of the sufficiency of the evidence to support the resolution of an issue by a trial judge or jury.

chapter 15

Choosing Between Competing Arguments — The Subjective Nature of Judicial Decisions

As you now know, for issues involving both rule application and rule creation, there are virtually always sound arguments "going both ways." As noted in Chapters 9 and 12, classroom dialogues will sometimes illustrate this point by requiring you or a colleague to articulate arguments for a result directly contrary to the result reached in a court opinion. Similarly, a professor may highlight the "both ways" phenomenon by posing a hypothetical and requiring you or a colleague to make arguments on both sides of an issue. This chapter addresses the nature of the decision courts must make when choosing between sound arguments on both sides of an issue.

I. A CHOICE BETWEEN COMPETING ARGUMENTS IS INHERENTLY SUBJECTIVE

A. Competing Legal Arguments Are Incommensurable

The arguments on each side of a rule application or a rule creation issue are incommensurable; that is, there is no generally agreed-on numerical scale, common denominator, or common metric that allows for a direct, objective comparison of the persuasive force or weight of the competing arguments. As a result, a judge making a decision on the merits on such issues is left with no alternative but to choose the argument(s) that in the judge's opinion are most persuasive. Thus, a decision applying an existing rule to a set of facts or creating a new legal rule is inherently subjective. To illustrate this incommensurability and resulting inherent subjectivity, we examine the case of *Lambert v. California*.

B. Background Information in *Lambert v. California*, 355 U.S. 225 (1957)

At the time of the *Lambert* decision, an ordinance in the City of Los Angeles required a convicted felon to register if present in the city for five days or more. Ms. Lambert was a convicted felon who failed to register in accordance with this ordinance. She was tried and convicted for violating the ordinance. On appeal, she claimed that the ordinance violated the Due Process Clause of the U.S. Constitution.

C. The Court's Opinion in *Lambert v. California*

Justice DOUGLAS delivered the opinion of the Court.

. . .

[The ordinance] provides that it shall be unlawful for "any convicted person" to be or remain in Los Angeles for a period of more than five days without registering; it requires any person having a place of abode outside the city to register if he comes into the city on five occasions or more during a 30-day period; and it prescribes the information to be furnished the Chief of Police on registering.

. . .

Appellant, arrested on suspicion of another offense, was charged with a violation of this registration law . . . The case was tried to a jury which found appellant guilty. The court fined her $250 and placed her on probation for three years.

. . . No element of willfulness is by terms included in the ordinance nor read into it by the California court as a condition necessary for a conviction.

We must assume that appellant had no actual knowledge of the requirement that she register under this ordinance, as she offered proof of this defense [at trial] which was refused [by the trial judge]. The question is whether a registration act of this character violates Due Process where it is applied to a person who has no actual knowledge of his duty to register, and where no showing is made of the probability of such knowledge.

. . . There is wide latitude on the lawmakers to declare an offense and to exclude elements of knowledge and diligence from its definition. . . . But we deal here with conduct that is wholly passive — mere failure to register. It is unlike the commission of acts, or the failure to act under circumstances that should alert the doer to the consequences of his deed. Cf. . . . United States v. Balint, 258 U.S. 250; United States v. Dotterweich, 320 U.S. 277, 284. The rule that "ignorance of the law will not excuse" . . . is deep in our law, as is the principle that of all the powers of local government, the police power is "one of the least limitable." On the other hand, Due Process places some limits on its exercise. Engrained in our concept of Due Process is the requirement of notice. Notice is sometimes essential so that the citizen has the chance to defend charges. Notice is required before property interests are disturbed, before assessments are made, before penalties are assessed. Notice is required in a myriad of situations where a penalty or forfeiture might be suffered for mere failure to act. Recent cases illustrating the point . . . involved only property interests in civil litigation. But the principle is equally appropriate where a person, wholly passive and unaware of any wrongdoing, is brought to the bar of justice for condemnation in a criminal case.

Registration laws are common and their range is wide. . . . Many such laws are akin to licensing statutes in that they pertain to the regulation of business activities. But the present ordinance is entirely different. Violation of its provisions is unaccompanied by any activity whatever, mere presence in the city being the test. Moreover, circumstances which might move one to inquire as to the necessity of registration are completely lacking . . . [T]his registrant on first becoming aware of her duty to register was given no opportunity to comply with the law and avoid its penalty, even though her default was entirely innocent. She could but suffer the consequences of the ordinance, namely, conviction with the imposition of heavy criminal penalties thereunder.

We believe that actual knowledge of the duty to register or proof of the probability of such knowledge and subsequent failure to comply are necessary before a conviction under the ordinance can stand. As Holmes wrote in *The Common Law*, "A law which punished conduct which would not be blameworthy in the average member of the community would be too severe for that community to bear." Id. at 50. Its severity lies in the absence of an opportunity either to avoid the consequences of the law or to defend any prosecution brought under it. Where a person did not know of the duty to register and where there was no proof of the probability of such knowledge, he may not be convicted consistently with Due Process. Were it otherwise, the evil would be as great as it is when the law is written in print too fine to read or in a language foreign to the community.

Reversed. . . .

Justice FRANKFURTER, whom Justice HARLAN and Justice WHITTAKER join, dissenting.

The present laws of the United States and of the forty-eight States are thick with provisions that command that some things not be done and others be done, although persons convicted under such provisions may have had no awareness of what the law required or that what they did was wrongdoing. The body of decisions sustaining such legislation, including innumerable registration laws, is almost as voluminous as the legislation itself. The matter is summarized in United States v. Balint, 258 U.S. 250, 252: "Many instances of this are to be found in regulatory measures in the exercise of what is called the police power where the emphasis of the statute is evidently upon achievement of some social betterment rather than the punishment of the crimes as in cases of mala in se."

. . . Considerations of hardship often lead courts, naturally enough, to attribute to a statute the requirement of a certain mental element — some consciousness of wrongdoing and knowledge of the law's command — as a matter of statutory construction. Then, too, a cruelly disproportionate relation between what the law requires and the sanction for its disobedience may constitute a violation of the Eighth Amendment as a cruel and unusual punishment, and, in respect to the States, even offend the Due Process Clause of the Fourteenth Amendment.

But what the Court here does is to draw a constitutional line between a State's requirement of doing and not-doing. What is this but a return to [outmoded] distinctions between feasance and nonfeasance — a distinction that may have significance in the evolution of common law notions of liability, but is inadmissible as a line between constitutionality and unconstitutionality. . . .

If . . . this decision were to be given its relevant scope, a whole volume of the United States Reports would be required to document in detail the legislation in this country that would fall or be impaired. I abstain from entering upon a consideration of such legislation, and adjudications upon it, because I feel confident that the present decision will turn out to be an isolated deviation from the strong current of precedents — a derelict on the waters of the law. Accordingly, I content myself with dissenting.

D. The Arguments Relied on by the Majority in *Lambert v. California*

The majority relies on at least two affirmative arguments to support the decision that the ordinance violates due process. These arguments might be seen as follows:

Argument #1 — Due process requires notice before property interests are disturbed, before assessments are made, and before penalties are assessed. This notice is required in a myriad of situations in which a civil penalty or civil forfeiture might be suffered for mere failure to act. The principle that due process requires notice is equally appropriate where a person, wholly passive and unaware of any wrongdoing, is charged in a criminal case.

This argument might be seen as a combination of principle argument (where a person is unaware that a failure to act involves criminal wrongdoing, due process generally requires notice to the person before the person can be charged with a crime) and an argument by analogy (such a notice has been required in analogous civil matters).

Argument #2 — The principle has been long established that the law should generally not punish conduct that would not be blameworthy in the average member of the community. An innocent failure to register would not be blameworthy in the average member of the community where a person does not know of the duty to register and where there has been no proof of the probability of such knowledge of such a duty. Therefore, striking down the ordinance is consistent with this principle.

This argument might be seen as a principle argument.

E. The Arguments Relied on by the Dissent in *Lambert v. California*

The dissent relies on at least two affirmative arguments to support the position that the ordinance does not violate due process. These arguments might be seen as follows:

Argument #1 — There are many current laws of the United States and of each State that have been upheld in court cases, including by the Supreme Court, in which persons convicted have had no awareness that what they did was wrong. Moreover, many of these laws were enacted under the police power, as the ordinance violated by Lambert.

This might be seen as an argument by analogy or an argument from precedent.

Argument #2 — The decision of the majority will call into question or invalidate a large number of similar registration laws throughout the country.

This might be seen as a principle argument (court decisions should generally not call into question numerous existing laws) or a consequences argument (this decision will produce the negative consequence of calling into question numerous existing laws).

F. The Competing Arguments of the Majority and Dissent Are Incommensurable and a Choice Between Them Is Subjective

The persuasive strength of the arguments by the majority and by the dissent cannot be directly compared. Argument #1 for the majority asserts that due process generally requires notice in analogous civil cases and should therefore require notice in this criminal case. Argument #1 for the dissent asserts that many other similar criminal statutes that do not require notice have previously been upheld by courts. Both of the arguments are sound. As you now know, courts routinely give weight to these types of arguments when reaching decisions, but there is no generally agreed-on way to convert the qualitative assessment of persuasive strength of each argument into a number (or other metric or ordinal designation) that allows for direct comparison of the persuasive strength of the arguments. Therefore, all a judge can do is make a subjective judgment about which argument, in the judge's opinion, carries greater persuasive force.

The inherently subjective nature of the assessment of the persuasive strength of arguments is not changed when each Argument #2 is added to the mix. These arguments are also incommensurable, whether considered alone or in conjunction with each respective Argument #1.

Because decisions resolving rule application issues and rule creation issues are subjective does not mean that these decisions are irrational or arbitrary. It is not irrational or arbitrary for courts to consider and subjectively assess the persuasive force of arguments based on goals, consequences, principles, analogies, precedents, and inferences when making legal decisions.

II. APPROACHES FOR MAKING THE SUBJECTIVE DECISION

Judges and other decision-makers might use one of the following two approaches when making subjective decisions about the persuasive force of competing arguments.

A. The Trumping Argument Approach

A decision-maker using this approach begins with a presumption that a particular argument should trump all competing arguments. For example, a judge may adopt a presumption that a goal or principle argument based on the "intent of the framers" should trump all other arguments and therefore determine the outcome in cases interpreting the U.S. Constitution. Trumping arguments are sometimes referred to as a judge's judicial philosophy.

In class discussions, a professor may also sponsor what she believes to be appropriate trumping arguments. For example, a professor might say or suggest that an argument based on the utilitarian principle of "do what is best for the largest number of people," or the economic principle of "do what is most efficient," should presumptively trump all competing arguments.

Judges and law professors may subscribe to a hard or soft trumping argument approach. Those subscribing to a hard trumping argument approach adopt an irrebuttable presumption that the trumping argument controls the outcome, e.g., in cases involving the interpretation of the

U.S. Constitution, a goal argument based on the intent of the framers should <u>always</u> be determinative. The soft approach would create a rebuttable presumption in favor of the trumping argument, e.g., in cases involving the interpretation of the U.S. Constitution, a goal argument based on the intent of the framers should <u>generally</u> control the outcome.

It may be quite reasonable for a decision-maker to use a trumping argument approach, especially if it is of the soft variety. But a trumping approach does not make decision-making objective. There are always sound arguments in favor of using any trumping argument and sound arguments in opposition to its use. These arguments are the same types of incommensurable arguments discussed throughout this book. Therefore, the arguments in support of, and in opposition to, any trumping argument approach are incommensurable. Consequently, the decision to rely on a particular trumping argument is an inherently subjective one.

B. The Open Competition Approach

A decision-maker using this approach considers all of the arguments on both sides of an issue, without invoking any presumptions in favor of a particular argument. After fully considering all of the arguments, the decision-maker reaches a decision. This decision necessarily finds one set of competing arguments more persuasive. Because the arguments are incommensurable, the ultimate decision is subjective.

C. Judges May Shift Between the Two Approaches

Judges may not always adhere to one of the foregoing two approaches. A judge might, for example, adopt a hard trumping argument approach for cases involving constitutional interpretation, a soft trumping argument approach for questions of statutory interpretation, and an open competition approach in negligence cases.

III. BALANCING — A MISLEADING METAPHOR

Court opinions or classroom discussions will sometimes indicate that the court reached a decision by "balancing" or "weighing" the competing arguments in a case. For example, a professor may develop arguments on both sides of an issue in class discussions, and then suggest that a court would have to reach a decision by "balancing" or "weighing" the competing arguments. This "balancing" and "weighing" language could tend to mislead you into believing that there is some generally agreed-on method for assigning some sort of numerical weight to competing arguments, and then objectively balancing them to determine the objectively correct or "right" answer. But since a final decision must choose between incommensurable arguments, the final decision is necessarily a subjective one.

IV. JUDICIAL DECISION-MAKING, LAW PRACTICE, AND EXAMS

Understanding the subjective nature of decisions resolving rule application and rule creation issues should help you in the practice of law. The subjective decision a judge is required to make means that a judge's background can easily influence a decision. A judge with a Ph.D. in economics, for example, may be strongly influenced by arguments based on principles of economics or consequences predicted by economic theories. If you know a judge's social, political, economic, educational, and employment background, you will be able to make informed strategic decisions about which arguments to emphasize and how to organize your arguments.[1]

Exam questions can sometimes focus on judicial decision-making. In a constitutional law course, for example, a professor might ask the following question:

> A U.S. Supreme Court Justice said that the rule of law requires that the intent of the framers control the outcome in cases interpreting the meaning of the U.S. Constitution. Comment.

Your answer to this type of question would require you to draw on class dialogues and course materials addressing approaches for judicial decision-making.

---

1. Many practicing lawyers routinely investigate the background of the judges before whom they will appear.

chapter 16

Helping Clients Make Decisions — Arguments Beyond the Courtroom

In law practice, clients will routinely ask you for advice about whether their proposed course of conduct is or is not "legal." Not all client questions are of the "**does the law permit me** to do this?" variety, however. When there are multiple alternatives for solving a problem, all of which are <u>permitted</u> under the law, clients will sometimes ask lawyers for advice about what course of action they *should* pursue. Consider just a few examples.

> You have advised your client that the law permits him to fire a current employee for misconduct. Your client asks you whether he *should* give the employee a warning or exercise his legal right to terminate the employee.

> You represent a labor union. The union's chief negotiator asks for your opinion about whether at this point in the negotiations with the employer she *should* reduce the amount of her demand for a wage increase or terminate the negotiations.

> Your client is a national environmental organization. The chief executive officer of the organization has identified several alternative positions the organization might take on pending federal clean air legislation. The officer asks you to help her decide which position the organization *should* take before Congress.

> You are counsel to the President of the United States. You have concluded that it is legal for the Untied States to take military action against another country to neutralize its alleged program for the development of weapons of mass destruction. The President asks for your advice about whether military action, economic sanctions or some other alternative *should* be the next course of action.

In each of the above examples, the client is faced with an important *should* decision. When clients ask for your assistance in making such decisions, you are put in the role of a counselor. One of your tasks in this role[1] is typically to help clients recognize that for such decisions, there are almost always arguments for and against each alternative course of action. Often these arguments are the conceptual clones of the arguments courts consider when applying and creating legal rules.

For instance, in the employee termination/warning example above, one of the client's **goals** might be to foster long-term commitment by employees. If so, before making a decision, a client might want to consider whether immediate termination of the employee might undermine that goal.

When advising the union negotiator, you would want to help the client identify likely unintended **consequences** of terminating negotiations. Might termination result in a loss of face by the employer's negotiator? If so, is that a positive or negative consequence? Answering such questions might bear on the decision to pursue or forego the termination alternative.

As a prelude to helping the environmental organization decide what position to take before Congress, you might want to investigate and then discuss with the client the positions taken by similar organizations with respect to **analogous** legislation proposed to Congress or state legislatures. The client's ultimate decision might well be informed by the positions taken and the results achieved in any such analogous situations.

When advising the President of the United States, you would want to help your client with a thorough consideration of at least the following: the country's foreign policy **goals**, the likely long- and short-term **consequences** of the alternative of military action, the **principles** that might arguably be established by or arguably violated by the alternative of military action, the results of military action in **analogous** circumstances, and the adequacy of the circumstantial evidence supporting any factual **inferences** about the presence or absence of weapons of mass destruction.

As these examples illustrate, when in your first year of law school you learn to make arguments and consider thoroughly the arguments on both sides of an issue, you are developing concepts and skills that you will routinely use in your role as a counselor in law practice.

---

1. For a detailed description of the process of counseling clients, see Binder, Bergman, Tremblay, and Price, *Lawyers as Counselors* (2d Ed, West 2004).

Index